STACK THE DECK

A step-by-step procedure for writing

Robert B. Cahill and Herbert J. Hrebic

edited by

Theresa Zigmond

ACKNOWLEDGMENTS

We would like to acknowledge the following students who contributed samples of their writing to serve as models: David Anderson, Bob Andorka, Julie Barcelona, Linas Bartuska, Tom Biskoski, Ed Bogus, Kurt Boras, Michael Bruhns, Marguerite Buck, Michael Bumann, Tom Christensen, Polly Cheroke, James Coppens, Charles Couper, John Crosetto, Joseph Crosetto, Phil Cyscon, Marius Daugirdas, Kathleen Driscoll, Terri Dunne, Joe Dyjak, Arnie Esquivel, Derrick Everett, Daniel Flens, Patricia Flynn, Chris Folga, Frank Grabowski, Oscar Hernandez, Michael Hogan, Tom Kelly, Richard Kennelly, Mark Krason, Mary Lenehan, Mary Lewandowski, Gintaras Lietuvninkas, Michael Lynch, Jennifer Marquardt, Martin Marren, Kevin Marzalik, Roshon May, Nancy McCory, Michael Miedlar, Kevin Moore, Chris Morton, Pat Mulligan, Frank Nolan, Mary O'Malley, Kazys Ozelis, Randy Pikowski, Rich Preng, Casey Ramas, Bill Rokaitis, Sarunas Rumsa, Dale Saunders, Cindy Savarise, Mark Schultz, Dan Shannon, Larry Sparks, David Stanczyk, Frank Suarez, Phil Vitaliano, Chris Vondrasek, Michael Wagner, Steve Wagner, Carl Wonderlick, Steve Wonderlick, Tom Woodrow, and David Zwierz.

We would also like to acknowledge the many people who helped in numerous ways: Don Augustyn, Jack Carlson, Marty Mongan, Marguerite Munk, Father Robert Sheridan, Patricia Sloper, John Mohan, John Fahey, Bishop James Keleher, Bill Hogan, Brother Hank Hammer, Bonnie Littleton, Mary Jane Cahill, Jan Mc Auliffe, Kathy Schmohe, Catherine Morrin, Frances Tenbroeck, Mary Ann Sheehan, and Stacey Zigmond.

A special note of thanks and appreciation to Theresa Zigmond who edited this book. Theresa has the patience of a saint to work with the shorter version of the Cahreb team.

ISBN 0-933282-25-7 paperback
ISBN 0-933282-26-5 hard cover

TABLE OF CONTENTS

To my partner, Bob,

always

Nobody taught you your native language. You have been using sentences since you uttered your first meaningful statement. Whether you were prodded from infancy by your parents to mimic words and phrases or whether you were left to your own devices, you gained operational control of English long before you started school.

You were undoubtedly able by the age of 4 or 5 to carry on a meaningful conversation with a wide variety of people, both children and adults. You were able to accomplish this feat because nature had equipped you with an amazing capacity to learn language without your even being aware of it.

From infancy you have taken note of the meaningful aspects of spoken language, made them your own, and have used them to communicate. You have learned the more than forty sounds of English and the rules for combining these to form words. You have mastered the many meanings of hundreds of words and also the relationships that exist among words.

You have become so expert at stringing words together in many sentence patterns that with the limited number of words you know, you are capable of creating an infinite number of sentences. You've done this quite naturally without formal instruction and without conscious effort.

YOU ARE A WALKING GRAMMAR! The knowledge of what makes language work and how it works is locked in your brain.

A sentence is any unit of language that communicates an idea. These ideas and communications range from very simple to very complex. These examples illustrate what we mean.

- Stop!
- Look out!
- Spencer burned the beans.
- Yolanda viewed Mount Shasta.
- While eating raw oysters at McCormick's Fish House, Sandra decided to visit London during her summer vacation.

SENTENCE SENSE

You have been using sentences like these without any conscious effort. The truth is that even before you started school, you were able to put words into patterns that allowed your listener to understand them. You did this quite naturally long before you were able to write or to label the parts of a sentence. The following drill should convince you that you do know how to construct sentences without having to name each part.

EXERCISE 1: Rearrange the following words into groups that make good *sentence sense.* Your word groupings should *sound* like sentences.

Example: sunlight tall green morning in the shimmered lush the trees.

Sentence: The tall, lush, green trees shimmered in the morning sunlight.

1. floor the boy sprang lazy to clumsily the.
2. toast Olivia her on French sugar sprinkles.
3. open graduate eager young the envelope ripped shouted and "More money!"
4. net ball smacked the soccer the Allan into.
5. Vegas won playing poker Shelby thousand three in dollars Las.

ORAL TO WRITTEN LANGUAGE

Realizing that you have oral control of language, the trick is to convert the control you have over spoken language to written language. Writing mirrors speech, but since it is learned and not automatic, we must consciously learn writing skills and techniques.

Don't panic! As you sorted the mixed up sets of words in the drill above, you used the natural process of sentence making, that is, you glued words together in meaningful strings without having to analyze them into parts of a sentence. You were using your natural control over language. You were putting words together rather than separating and tagging them. Being able to underline verbs and circle nouns or identify gerunds and past participles has nothing to do with writing.

Just as the beginning dancer must learn to manipulate her feet consciously in preconceived patterns to create smooth movement, so the beginning writer must learn to manipulate words and sentences in *stacked* patterns to create impact through word flow.

WRITER'S VOCABULARY

All great writers have learned the secret of packaging their ideas to create impact upon their readers. Anyone can become a good writer if she learns to master the skills of language manipulation.

This mastery involves the learning of four writing skills: **combining**, **rearranging**, **subtracting**, and **expanding**. An almost unlimited number of options are available to a writer once she has mastered these skills.

You automatically use these four skills when you speak. Combine the four sentences *orally* into one sentence.

1. There is a pig.
2. The pig wallowed.
3. There is a puddle.
4. The puddle is muddy.

Spontaneously, you probably said one of the following sentences:

1. The pig wallowed in the muddy puddle or (mud puddle).
2. There is a pig wallowing in a mud puddle.
3. The pig wallowed in the puddle which is muddy.
4. A pig is wallowing in the muddy puddle.

Your brain, the greatest computer in the world, automatically used all four manipulatory skills.

1. You **combined** four sentences into one.

2. You **rearranged** words, perhaps putting *mud* before *puddle*.

3. You **subtracted** unnecessary words. There were 15 words in the original four sentences. How many words did you use?

4. You **expanded** with words that were not included in the original four sentences. Maybe you used the word *in* or the word *which*.

The second reason we teach these skills is even more important. These four oral language skills must become part of your **writer's vocabulary** that you can use in writing assignments in all of your classes.

SUMMARY

You must learn how to **combine** ideas, so that you can write a variety of sentence openings and structures in your compositions.

You must learn how to **rearrange** words, so that you can position important words in key places to emphasize ideas. In other words, you must learn to create impact for your audience.

You must learn how to **subtract**, so that you do not clutter your writing with unnecessary and repeated words and ideas.

You must learn how to **expand**, so that you support your statements with specific details, examples, and reasons.

You will learn these skills as you function with them.   Don't worry if you cannot identify direct objects, present participles, or gerunds for these exercises.

COMBINING IDEAS

The combining of sentences is the beginning of conscious control of word flow. You control word flow. As a writer, you decide which word comes first, second, third, etc. You decide how many sentences you will combine. You decide if you will combine at all. Thus, word flow is your conscious control over how you will communicate to your audience.

All sentences are constructed of **idea words** and **glue words**.

Idea words function as nouns, pronouns, verbs, adjectives, adverbs, and interjections. They present thoughts and ideas.

Glue words function as articles or determiners, coordinating or subordinating conjunctions, and as prepositions. In the sentence, *A small boy fell into the pond and swam to safety*, the idea words are: *small*, *boy*, *fell*, *pond*, *swam*, and *safety*. The glue words are: *a*, *into*, *the*, *and*, and *to*.

Notice in the following example that the six sentences have been combined in nine different ways. The possibilities of combining ideas are almost unlimited. You will improve your writing style as you begin to master the skill of combining.

Example: There is a boy. The boy is small. There is a pond.
                The boy fell.   The boy swam.   The boy is safe.

1. A small boy fell into the pond and swam to safety.
2. The small boy swam to safety despite a fall into the pond.
3. Into the pond the small boy fell and swam to safety.
4. The small boy fell into the pond, but he swam to safety.
5. Swimming to safety was the small boy who had fallen into the pond.
6. The small boy who fell into the pond swam to safety.
7. Falling into the pond and swimming to safety was the small boy.
8. The small boy who swam to safety had fallen into the pond.
9. To safety swam the small boy who had fallen into the pond.

Notice how the **IMPACT** or emphasis on ideas is changed by how the sentence is arranged. Find the sentence where the impact is on the idea that *the boy was able to swim to safety.* Certainly, you could think of even more arrangements than there are listed here. Try them.

When you speak, you use different types of words to combine ideas. Without knowing their definition, you automatically use subordinating conjunctions, relative pronouns, and verbals. Now you need to convert those oral skills to written language.

EXERCISE 1: Combine each of the following sentences in two different ways using **glue words** (subordinating conjunctions), **WH words** (relative pronouns), and/or **ING words** (gerunds and present participles).

Glue Words:	**subordinating conjunctions:** after, although, when, since, because, as, where, if, before, until, so that, though, unless, as soon as, even though, etc.
WH Words:	**relative pronouns**: who, whom, whose, which, **that**. (There are always exceptions in the English language.)
ING Words:	**gerund**: ING Word which acts like a noun-- "**Swimming** is a good exercise." **present participle:** ING word which acts like an adjective-- "The turtle chased the **swimming** boy."

After you have written your sentences, read them aloud to your partner or your small group to hear if they are "well-formed."

Example: Mrs. Ima Crouch **was** upset.
She had **assigned** Sam a composition.
The composition **contained** sentence fragments.

   • Mrs. Ima Crouch was upset **because** the paper Sam wrote contained
      sentence fragments. (subordinating conjunction = glue word)
   • Sam, **who** wrote a paper with fragments in it, upset Mrs. Ima Crouch.
      (relative pronoun = WH word)
   • **Upsetting** Mrs. Ima Crouch, Sam wrote a composition containing
      fragments. (present participle = ING word)

1. Suzy **teaches** English.
    She **loves** to read. (because, who, ing)

2. Billie Jo Bujnowski **lives** in Grand Rapids.
    He **attends** Wyoming High School. (ing, who, because)

3. Cameron **hung** from the tree.
    He **held** two bunches of bananas in his teeth.

4. The enthusiastic Bulls' fans **jumped** to their feet.
    They **screamed** with delight.

5. Jeremy **took** a test.
    His test **earned** an "A."
    He **jumped** over the fence.
    He **shouted**, "Yaahoo!"

6. MiKyung Mc Nerney **liked** to dance.
    She **whirled** around the floor.
    She **became** very dizzy.

7. Sophomores **have** trouble writing papers.
    Mr. Stachofsky **is** their teacher.
    He **suffers**.

8. Storms **swept** the Colorado countryside.
    Constance **grows** tomatoes.
    The tomatoes **were ruined.**

9. There **is** a goalie.
    The goalie **is** scrappy.
    There **is** a ball.
    The ball **is spinning**.
    The goalie **traps** the ball.

10. Felix **meowed**.
    Felix **meowed** loudly.
    Felix **paced**.
    Felix **paced** angrily.
    There **was** no food.
    There **was** a dish.
    The dish **was** empty.

REARRANGING IDEAS

Now that you practiced combining sentences into longer ones, you will understand that you can create IMPACT upon your audience by the word flow that you choose. Rearrangement of these already combined sentences can help you understand how word flow works.

Rearranging sentences will help you express your ideas in a variety of ways. Also, rearranging will help you avoid a common writing problem, that is, a lack of variety in sentence openings and sentence structures.

Too many students tend to begin their sentences with the repetition of *I, The, And,* and *Then* and to repeat the common subject-verb-object (S-V-O) sentence structure.

One of the advantages of the written word is that it is permanent. Therefore, it lends itself to rearranging ideas and varying sentence openings and structures.

Discuss how the emphasis on ideas changes in the following examples when the sentence is rearranged. Before you do some on your own, do several of the exercise sentences together as a class to practice emphasizing different ideas.

Example:

    a. Sidney left for the bus stop twenty minutes early the first day of school, hoping that he was going to the right bus stop.

    b. The first day of school Sidney left twenty minutes early for what he hoped was the right bus stop.

    c. Hoping he was going to the right bus stop, Sidney left the house twenty minutes early the first day of school.

    d. Twenty minutes early Sidney left for the bus stop on the first day of school, so he could find the right bus stop.

EXERCISE 2: Rearrange the following sentences so that you can see the various ways of packaging ideas for creating different effects.

    1. Jumping off the roof while holding an umbrella, Juanita broke her leg.

    2. The hot air balloon lurched wildly as it climbed into the sky.

3. Jesse fell and broke his arm while trying to build a birdhouse in a maple tree on a hot, July afternoon.

4. The explosion at the "We Stuff 'Em, You Fluff 'Em" pillow factory on a windy November afternoon created quite a widespread problem.

5. Meg, brushing her long, black hair, sang happily.

6. Salvatore Ferragamo was saddened because of so many disappointments.

7. Maurice screamed hysterically.

8. Leroy Bowen shouted a friendly greeting walking into the choir loft.

9. Cautiously Tina Zuccolo fingered the ball before glancing down for the sign from Missy Keyes.

10. Ethel looked up the information in the encyclopedia.

11. Dr. I. Yankum reached into the patient's mouth and forcefully grasped the bubble gum.

12. The football coach paced relentlessly along the sidelines.

13. Shanita yawned sleepily, rolled over, and adjusted her pillow just as the ceiling fell down.

14. As lightning streaked across the sky, Irving hid under the covers.

15. Risnosnick Obenglobben Fuffarachack Aruttneputtanich Nockensnopel lunged quickly and tackled the burglar.

REARRANGING TO EMPHASIZE KEY IDEAS

Another way to emphasize key ideas is to place words out of their usual order. This repositioning of words jars the reader by making her pause from reading sentence patterns in the normal order to which she is accustomed. Notice the difference in emphasis in the following two sentences:

> Dr. N. O. Payne drilled relentlessly **into Pepi's tooth**.
>
> **Into Pepi's tooth** Dr. N.O. Payne drilled relentlessly.

Discuss the difference in emphasis in these two sentences. Which sentence emphasizes the word *relentlessly* the most? What about *into Pepi's tooth*?

Adjectives normally come before the words they modify. However, by repositioning the adjectives *after* the word, a different emphasis results. Study the following two sentences.

A **tall, dark, handsome** stranger appeared in the doorway.
A stranger, **tall, dark, and handsome**, appeared in the doorway.

EXERCISE 3: Rearrange the following sentences, putting words out of their normal order. Do the first two as a group activity. You might also change the form of a word.

1. I could not accept Rocky's excuse.

2. Cousin Tommy is happy-go-lucky and witty, and he keeps the guys on their toes during fishermen's weekend.

3. Michael Jordan's body skied forward, propelled by the springs in his legs.

4. The sun was blazing yellow and was glorious.

5. I studied the unit thoroughly the night before, and I wasn't worried about Mr. Rychtarik's quiz.

6. The spirited, little baby crawled fiercely across the patio floor.

7. Maggie is an excellent seamstress, and she shops shrewdly for bargains.

8. The fierce, cold winds began to blow, causing the waves to rise above the breaker.

9. The heroine's most admirable trait is her courage in the face of difficulty.

10. The coach is a fair individual, but she will not accept the reporter's criticism.

USING THE SKILLS OF COMBINING AND REARRANGING TO REVISE A COMPOSITION

One of the more difficult skills to learn is to revise a composition. For many students, revision simply means writing in ink instead of pencil and/or correcting spelling, punctuation, or capitalization mistakes. The writer's vocabulary skills of **combining** and **rearranging** can help you improve your sentence structures and openings.

EXERCISE 4: Read through the following models several times to become familiar with the content. Then rewrite each story using your skills of **combining** and **rearranging** to vary sentence openings and sentence structures.

Remember to use subordinating conjunctions and prepositions (glue words), relative pronouns (WH words), and present participles (ING words). In other words, make this story as good an example of writing as you possibly can.

Example:

1. Francois was a soldier. 2. He was short. 3. He was fat. 4. He weighed more than 300 pounds. 5. He wore a beard. 6. It was black. 7. It was bushy. 8. It covered 3/4 of his face.

> Weigh**ing** more than 300 pounds, Francois, a short, fat soldier, wore a black, bushy beard, **which** covered 3/4 of his face.

> Francois, **who** wore a black, bushy beard covering 3/4 of his face, was a short, fat soldier, weigh**ing** more than 300 pounds.

Francois, the Soldier

1. Francois was a soldier. 2. He was short. 3. He was fat. 4. He weighed more than 300 pounds. 5. He wore a beard. 6. It was black. 7. It was bushy. 8. It covered 3/4 of his face. 9. He had eyes. 10. They were beady. 11. They were black. 12. They peered out from sockets. 13. The sockets were deep. 14. They were hollow. 15. He had a nose. 16. It was balloon like. 17. He had coarse, black bristles. 18. They sprouted out of his nose. 19. The nose was rough. 20. It was red. 21. Francois was a braggart. 22. He was a liar. 23. He fabricated stories. 24. He told them in saloons. 25. He loved audiences. 26. He had a favorite story. 27. He stopped twenty soldiers. 28. He did it. 29. They were crossing a bridge. 30. It was a secret bridge. 31. It led into the city. 32. It wasn't guarded. 33. Francois saved Cleveland. 34. Believe this story. 35. He will tell another.

The Escape

1. There was a grocery store. 2. Danny backed out. 3. He carried a gun. 4. He fired a shot into the air. 5. He whirled about. 6. There was an alley. 7. It was pitch dark. 8. He leaped. 9. He ran. 10. He ran fast. 11. He ran faster and faster. 12. There were rocks. 13. He tripped. 14. There was a garbage can. 15. He bumped. 16. He spun around. 17. There was cement. 18. He stumbled. 19. He was dazed. 20. He was dizzy. 21. He picked himself up. 22. He started to run. 23. He had to escape. 24. He just had to. 25. He tripped again. 26. He stumbled again. 27. He was blind. 28. Bats are blind. 29. He was tired. 30. He was terribly tired. 31. There was ground. 32. He dropped. 33. He tried. 34. He picked himself up. 35. He just couldn't. 36. He crawled forward. 37. He collapsed. 38. He lay there. 39. He was face down. 40. There was dust.

A Frightening Incident

1. There was a forest. **2.** Gloom shrouded the forest. **3.** There was a path.
4. It was narrow. **5.** It zigzagged into the darkness. **6.** There was a mansion.
7. It was old. **8.** It stood through the trees. **9.** There were weeds. **10.** They were tall.
11. They surrounded the mansion. **12.** There were bushes. **13.** They were untrimmed.
14. They surrounded the mansion. **15.** There was smoke. **16.** It was a wisp. **17.** It was thin. **18.** It curled from the chimney. **19.** It curled. **20.** The curl was lazy. **21.** The chimney was vine smothered. **22.** No sign of life appeared. **23.** There was thunder. **24.** It was low. **25.** It was rumbling. **26.** It gave a warning. **27.** It warned of a storm. **28.** The storm would come. **29.** It would come soon. **30.** There was a girl scout troop. **31.** It was Troop 7740. **32.** They sought shelter. **33.** They entered the house. **34.** The house was old. **35.** There was a gust. **36.** It was of wind. **37.** It was great. **38.** It blew through the window. **39.** It slammed the door violently. **40.** There was a light. **41.** It was dim. **42.** It filtered into the lower hallway. **43.** Shrieks filled the air. **44.** Wails filled the air. **45.** They were wild. **46.** There was a face. **47.** It was ugly. **48.** It appeared over the staircase. **49.** It held a candle. **50.** It lurked in the distance. **51.** They were terrified. **52.** They were bewildered. **53.** There was a wall. **54.** They groped their way. **55.** Their way was along the wall. **56.** They searched for a door. **57.** Minutes passed. **58.** They found the knob. **59.** They twisted it. **60.** It opened readily. **61.** They were surprised. **62.** A blast of air struck their faces. **63.** It was cool. **64.** It was night. **65.** There was a trail. **66.** It was winding. **67.** They fled down the trail. **68.** They did not glance backward.

The Cave

1. I entered the cave. **2.** The entrance was on the northwest side. **3.** The opening was small. **4.** I managed to squeeze through. **5.** I saw a huge chamber. **6.** It was full of walls. **7.** The walls were colorless. **8.** It was full of boulders. **9.** They weighed tons. **10.** I began walking. **11.** I reached the main chamber. **12.** Dozens of passages led from it. **13.** I went down the largest. **14.** I noticed many things. **15.** These things frightened me. **16.** Lizards darted about. **17.** Fluid oozed from the corner. **18.** Shadowy images were on the walls. **19.** I continued further. **20.** I saw a pile of white bones. **21.** A ropelike moss hung dangling in the air. **22.** My blood ran cold. **23.** I turned around. **24.** I wanted to run back. **25.** The passage stood no more. **26.** It was only solid rock. **27.** I began to scream. **28.** I ran past the pile of bones. **29.** It stood in front of me. **30.** It was the end of the cave.

USING THE SENTENCE OPENING SHEET TO REVISE

Once your first draft is completed, go back and number your sentences. Then you may fill out the **Sentence Opening Sheet** (SOS). This device will enable you to check for common student writing errors. For example, it will help you check to see if your sentences all begin with the same repetitious sentence openings. It will also enable you to check for verb tense consistency and concrete and active verbs. It will also help you to check for short, choppy sentences and run-on sentences. In short, it is a practical solution to many student writing problems.

Column One   **First Four Words Per Sentence**

Write in the first four words of each sentence. Check to see if your sentences begin with the same openings. If they do, you need to apply the skills of combination and rearrangement.

Also, if your sentences begin with a subordinating conjunction (glue word), read that sentence to see if it is a fragment.

A good way to check for fragments in paragraphs is to read the paper *aloud* backwards one sentence at a time. Begin with the last sentence and stop. Does it make sense? Reading aloud helps you to hear incomplete thoughts.

Look at the following example:

Example: **1.** I wore my heavy sweater to school.   **2. Because** it was cold.

Which group of words is a fragment? When you are reading forward, you might not hear the fragment because your mind combines sentences. By reading backwards one sentence at a time and pausing after each one, you can hear the fragment.

If you still cannot tell if your sentences makes sense, pull out a 3 x 5 card with the words:

I BELIEVE THAT

Read the words **I Believe That** *before* the sentence you are checking. If the sentence sounds okay, it's probably a complete thought. If it sounds confusing, it is probably a fragment.

13

Column Two   Special

This column can be used for a variety of items. If your teacher wanted you to emphasize the use of subordinating conjunctions, for example, you would list each subordinating conjunction used in the paragraph. Sometimes teachers label this column as "Pet Peeves" or "Dead Words," e.g., *nice, stuff, very, thing, you know, I think, alot,* oops, *a lot,* etc.

If these "Pet Peeve" words appear on your first draft, substitute more specific words.

Column Three   Verbs

Verb tense consistency is important. Therefore, we will use the verb column to check not only what verbs are used, but also the tense of each verb. The verbs should all be in the **past** tense for this assignment. Each main verb is written on its own line even if the sentence has more than one main verb. Be sure to include any helping verbs with the main verb. You can also use the verb column to see if you have repeated the same verbs over and over. Remember **VP**. That's **Verb Power**.

Example: Herbert **confessed** to the crime. The word *confessed* is listed in column three.

Special Hint: Do not forget that ING words must have a helping verb in order to act like real verbs. Also, *to* plus a verb (infinitive phrase) is not behaving like a verb, so you do not list them in the verb column.

If you have a difficult time identifying verbs, write the phrase **He** or **She**_____ above the verb column on the **Sentence Opening Sheet**. Read your verb with **He or She**_____. If it makes sense, it is probably the verb in the sentence.

Examples: He <u>swimming</u>.   **no verb**
                  He <u>is</u> <u>swimming</u>.   **verb**

                  She <u>tall</u>.   **no verb**
                  She <u>is</u> tall.   **verb**

Count the number of words you used in each sentence. First, if the sentences are all about the same length, you may need to combine and/or rearrange them for the sake of variety.

Second, if you have a very low number of words (3, 4, or 5), you need to make sure that the sentence is not a fragment. On the other hand, if your sentence is very long (20 or more words), you should check to make sure that it is not a run-on sentence.

Rules for identifying and correcting run-ons are listed on page **51**.

EXCHANGING SENTENCE OPENING SHEETS

Your teacher may ask one or two volunteers to share **Sentence Opening Sheets** with the class on the overhead projector. Or he may ask you to exchange SOS sheets with a partner(s) so that you can help analyze each other's paper.

After you have carefully studied your completed SOS sheet, you will want to make notes on the bottom of the sheet indicating what changes you plan to make. Next, you will want to make the corrections on the first draft itself. Skipping lines leaves room to insert the changes you have decided upon.

As you are rewriting your first draft, be aware of your **Sentence Opening Sheet**. Be sure to include in your final draft all the corrections you indicated on the bottom of your **Sentence Opening Sheet**.

Be especially careful of variety in your sentence openings, fragments because of transitions or relative pronoun openings, consistency in verb tenses, repetition of the same weak verbs, short, choppy sentences, or run-on sentences.

Name_____**Period**_____

Sentence Openings (first 4 words)	Special	Verbs	#
			of Words
		He____	

SUPPLEMENTAL EXERCISE

EXERCISE 5: Before writing your final draft, complete the following exercise on fragments and run-ons to help you avoid similar errors in your own paper. Correct the errors by using your skills of combination and rearrangement. Also, make sure all the verbs are in the past tense.

Fragment :   Francois, a short, fat soldier who weighed more than 300 pounds. **Wearing** a black, bushy beard **which** covered 3/4 of his face.

Corrected :   A short, fat soldier weighing more than 300 pounds, Francois wore a black, bushy beard covering 3/4 of his face.

Run-On :   Twisting the knob, they flung open the **door they** fled into the cold air which struck their faces.

Corrected :   Twisting the knob, they flung open the door and fled into the cold air which struck their faces.

Francois

1. Francois, the short, fat soldier who weighed more than 300 pounds. Wearing a black, bushy beard. Which covers most of his face.
2. He had black beady eyes they looked like they peer out from hollow sockets.
3. Francois, the lying braggart, always fabricates stories. Especially when he has one favorite story to tell everyone.
4. His big, bushy beard covering 3/4 of his face. His eyes, small, black, and beady peering out from those deep, hollow sockets.
5. Francois, a braggart and liar, fabricates stories he loved to tell them in front of large audiences.

The Escape

1. Carrying a gun, Dan backing out and firing a shot in the air.
2. Dizzy and dazed, he picks himself up he starts running.
3. Stumbling blindly, he tripped again he couldn't stop.
4. Running in complete darkness as fast as he could.
5. As he was running. He trips over rocks and bumped into garbage cans.

A Frightening Incident

1. A figure holding a candle with an ugly face that appeared over the staircase. Which lurked in the distance.
2. Minutes passed before they found the knob as they twist the knob the door opened readily.
3. Surrounded by tall weeds and untrimmed bushes. An old mansion stood through the trees.
4. They find the knob they twisted it open readily. As a blast of cool night air strikes their faces.
5. Seeking shelter a girl scout troop which entered the old mansion.

The Cave

1. As I squeeze through the small opening. I saw a huge chamber full of colorless walls.
2. Walking through the main chamber, I reach dozens of passages I went down the largest. Where I noticed many things.
3. Lizards darting about and fluid oozing from the corner.
4. The passage stood no more it is only solid rock.
5. I begin to scream. As I passed a pile of bones. Which stood in front of me.

FINAL DRAFT

In rewriting your paper, you should correct all the mistakes from the first draft. The **Sentence Opening Sheet** and your partner's help should have made you aware of any errors you had on your first draft.

Try to make your final draft error-free. Show your **PRIDE**!

Special Hint: Besides reading your own paper aloud, have a proofreading partner read your paper. Quite often this will help you hear mistakes which you otherwise might have missed.

Here are some questions to ask yourself as you reread your final draft.

1. Have I combined and rearranged?
2. Have I varied my sentence openings?
3. Did I correct any fragments because of glue word openings?
4. Did I eliminate all teacher "pet peeves" or "dead words"?
5. Did I write all my verbs in the past tense?
6. Did I check to see if any of my overly long sentences are run-ons?
7. Did I vary my sentence lengths?

PUBLISHING

In rewriting your draft, correct all mechanical errors. Your **Sentence Opening Sheet** should have helped you with your sentence openings and structures.

Besides reading your paper aloud, have a proofreading partner read your paper. Finally, some students might volunteer to read their final drafts in front of the class.

SUMMARY

Combining and **rearranging** are important skills to use in composing and revising a first draft. Here are some checklist questions to use with these **writer's vocabulary** skills:

1. Do I repeat the same dull openings, e.g., *I, The, And then, And so,* etc.?

2. Which sentences can I **combine** to make them more interesting for my audience by varying my sentence openings?

3. Which sentences can I **rearrange** to avoid repeating the same dull openings?

4. Am I emphasizing key ideas by placing them in a position of importance at the beginning or end of a sentence?

In **Unit 2** you practiced the first two writer's vocabulary skills-- **combining** and **rearranging**. Now you will be introduced to the skills of **subtracting** and **expanding**, which will also help you revise a composition.

Sometimes students "pad" their sentences by adding empty words that contribute nothing to the meaning of the sentence. These extra words clutter sentences and prevent the writers from communicating their ideas clearly.

Instead of being concise, students will write as many words as possible. Apparently they think that more words add up to a higher grade. **YUK!** Try to remember that $2 + 2 = 5$ does not add up to a higher grade in math either! Here are some space fillers to avoid:

Space Fillers

on account of the fact that	what I want to say
in spite of the fact that	all things being equal
due to the fact that	all of a sudden
needless to say	what I mean is
this paper will	as I said previously
WH Word clauses (which . . ., who . . .,)	In the following three paragraphs I intend to prove . . .

Inexperienced writers will also write in circles by repeating words or ideas. For example, in the sentence, *Byron Bronson thought in his mind how he could finagle a passing grade in Chemistry 102 from Ms. Dinklemaker,* doesn't the writer add unnecessary words by including the expression *in his mind*? It is only logical that Byron would think *in his mind*.

SUBTRACTING UNNECESSARY WORDS AND IDEAS

EXERCISE 1: Rewrite the following sentences, subtracting the unnecessary words or repeated ideas. Study the examples first. Complete the first three sentences as a group activity.

Example: Zelda Beldwood did not finish writing her letter to Myron

Marsynkowski **on account of the fact that** she broke her little finger.

Revised: Zelda Beldwood did not finish writing her letter to Myron Marsynkowski because she broke her little finger.

Example: **What I mean is that** you better start using the Sentence Opening Sheet to revise your first drafts or you'll fail English.

Revised: Start using the Sentence Opening Sheet to revise your first drafts or you'll fail English.

1. What I want to do is buy a pontoon boat to motor up Lake Poygan during my summer vacation.

2. What Jessica wants is to attend St. Mary's College, which is a private school located in South Bend, Indiana.

3. On account of the fact that Stacey wanted to earn extra money to pay for her college tuition, she worked at Hackney's Hamburger Joint over the holidays.

4. In spite of the fact that he would gain extra weight and would not be able to fit into his new Jordache jeans, Pat Cahill kept on eating pasta three meals a day.

5. The man who was swimming in the lake was bitten by a turtle, which was a snapping turtle.

6. I saw with my eyes that G. W. Whatley had scored the winning touchdown in spite of the fact that the instant replay referee ruled against G. W. Whatley's scoring the winning touchdown.

7. I shall never forget my first date with Eloise Pulinski on account of the fact that her dad stared me down when I came to pick her up on our first date.

8. Sometimes a loser who loses a game gains more than a winner, who wins the game at the loser's expense.

9. Until right before the moment that I began my very first speech in speech class, I had not felt very nervous and anxious and full of anxiety about my first speech.

10. A chill wind, which was icy, swept across the dark and dreary room, which was filled with lockers, after the terrible defeat and loss to our rivals, the Gompers Geoducks.

SUBTRACTING UNNECESSARY WORDS IN A COMPOSITION

EXERCISE 2: Rewrite the following student composition, subtracting unnecessary words or ideas. Complete this in cooperative learning groups.

1. On the first day of school it is easy to recognize freshmen on account of the fact that some are nervous and others are cocky. **2.** The students who are nervous can be easily detected because they are the ones who appear fidgety because of the fact that they can be seen studying room numbers and schedules. **3.** Also they are the ones who are milling outside their first class of the day before the first bell rings, or they can be seen carrying all their books for all their classes even the classes they have in the afternoon.

4. The cocky students come to the new school with clothes which are new and they come to school on the first day well prepared for the start of the new school year. **5.** They approach the faculty with very, many questions which are curious. **6.** They are also the ones who have a smugness on their faces. **7.** Because of the freshmen's outward appearance, it is easy to spot the different types on the first day of school at the beginning of the new school year.

EXPANDING IDEAS

Another common writing problem is that inexperienced writers tend to be vague and general instead of supplying the audience with specific information. One way to avoid this is to expand general ideas by using the journalistic questions: **Who**? **What**? **Why**? **Where**? **When**? **How**? For example, in the sentence, *The teacher complained about the student's behavior,* the reader does not know *who* the teacher is, *who* the student is, *what* the behavior was, or *how* the teacher complained.

In the following sentence how has the writer expanded by answering the journalistic questions *who, what,* and *how*?

Example: Mr. Michael McWhiz, the biology teacher, complained bitterly about Mary
            Ellen Snodgrass's dunking Billy Shapiro's sweater into the fish tank.

EXERCISE 3: Using the journalistic questions, **expand** the following general sentences into more specific ones. Share your expansions with your partner or group when you finish.

1. Everyone was excited about the tournament. **Who? How? When?**
2. The girl loves the dentist's drill. **Who? What? Why?**
3. The game was thrilling. **What game? Why? When?**
4. She sang nicely.
5. He liked his boat.
6. They are fixing a car.
7. The children are building.
8. She made a sundae.
9. He said.
10. It sounded strange.

EXERCISE 4: Expand the ideas by answering the journalistic questions *who, what, why, where, when, how.* Certain questions can be asked more than once while others may not be used at all. To begin, use only three journalistic questions for each idea to avoid creating long, awkward sentences. If you think you can handle more than three questions, go ahead and try it, as long as your sentences make sense. After you write your first sentence with the expanded ideas, rearrange it so that the second sentence begins with a different opening.

Example: The teacher lectured the freshman.

Who   **Mr. Chaucer, the new composition teacher,** lectured the **skinny little freshman.**

What   Mr. Chaucer, the new composition teacher, **glared** down his nose **as he lectured** the skinny, little freshman.

Why   Mr. Chaucer, the new composition teacher, glared down his nose as he lectured the skinny, little freshman **about writing on the desk.**

Where   Mr. Chaucer, the new composition teacher **in room #10**, glared down his nose as he lectured the skinny, little freshman about writing on the desk.

23

When   Mr. Chaucer, the new composition teacher in room #10, glared down his nose as he lectured the skinny, little freshman he had kept **after class** about writing on the desk.

How   Mr. Chaucer, the new composition teacher in room #10, glared down his nose as he **grumpily** lectured the skinny little freshman he had kept after class about writing on the desk.

Remember to try different openings after you have written the first expansion. Like this:

- **Lecturing grumpily** about writing on the desk, Mr. Chaucer kept the skinny, little freshman after class.

- **The new composition teacher** in room #10, Mr. Chaucer, kept the skinny, little freshman after class to lecture him about writing on the desk.

- **Because the skinny** little freshman had written on the desk, Mr. Chaucer kept him after class for a grumpy lecture.

1. In the attic	**6.** Paul flirts
2. Walter flunked	**7.** Fluffy chased the dog
3. Heidi volleys	**8.** Walking in the park
4. To answer the phone	**9.** Jean ditched
5. Aggie shopped	**10.** Basking in the sun

SUMMARY

Two new words were added to your writer's vocabulary. **Subtracting** enables you to eliminate unnecessary or repeated words or ideas that bore your audience. **Expanding** enables you to support your statements with specific reasons, details, and examples.

As you are revising your compositions, ask yourself these questions:

1. Are there any unnecessary words or repeated ideas in my sentences?
2. Did I feel up my paper with empty words to fill up space?
3. Can I make my writing more interesting for my audience by expanding my ideas with journalistic questions?
4. Where do I need to provide more information for my audience?

The dictionary defines *purpose* as *intention, aim, resolution, determination, reason for doing something.* Just as we each have different purposes for what we do, so writers have different purposes for the writing they do.

Every writer has a reason for writing. The reasons might be to persuade, to explain, to give directions, to entertain, or to reveal feelings. In any case, each of us needs to determine how we will write by thinking about whom it is we want to read our writing and why we want them to read it. In other words, we decide **PURPOSE** and **AUDIENCE**. For example, if you were describing your new boyfriend, Bruno Theophyllis, you certainly would not write the same way to your Aunt Josephine as you would to your best friend Sophie Iliakis.

Example:	Topic:	boyfriend, Bruno Theophyllis
	Purpose:	to describe him
	Audience:	Aunt Josephine
	Sentence:	Bruno Theophyllis is a nice, well-mannered young man from a good Greek family.

Example:	Topic:	boyfriend, Bruno Theophyllis
	Purpose:	to show your feelings about Bruno
	Audience:	Sophie Iliakis, best friend
	Sentence:	My heart pounds and my voice gets choked up when Bruno whispers, "Annamarie."

What are the differences between the two sentences? How are the words Annamarie uses different for each purpose and audience?

All of your life you have been adjusting your language to fit your purpose and your audience in your oral communications. Now you have to make the same adjustment in your writing.

EXERCISE 1: As a class, discuss the different ideas you might include for the following topics based on the purpose and the audience.

1. Topic: unfinished math homework assignment
   Audiences: math teacher and classmates at the cafeteria table

2. Topic: wanting to get a raise from your boss for your part-time job
   Audiences: parents and the boss

CONTROLLING IDEA

Now that you have the idea of the writer's purpose and how it is limited, it is time to go to the next step. After you have decided exactly what you will write about, you must decide how to get the message to your audience, the reader. The most common way to express your purpose is in a controlling idea, sometimes called a topic sentence.

A controlling idea/topic sentence is a contract which you make with your audience. It contains the **topic** that you are writing about and the **key words** which limit and direct how you will develop the topic. Here are two examples of student controlling ideas:

Controlling Idea:

                           t
Catching a steelhead trout requires
   kw   **kw**   **kw**
strength, patience, and **know-how.**

Can you make lists for each key word? If you cannot, you would be unable to write this paper. List-making is a necessary prerequisite in the prewriting stage of the writing process.

Controlling Idea:

                           t
My eighty-five-year-old grandmother
             kw   **kw**
reads comic books, rides motorcycles,
        kw
and **eats anchovy-covered pizza.**

Can you give specific examples of grandmother's unusual activities? If you cannot, you should select a different topic.

BEING AN AUDIENCE

Good writers write with a purpose for a specific audience. In order to understand how those two things operate, you need to practice being an audience.

Pretend you are the audience for **EXERCISE 2**'s well-written controlling ideas/topic sentences by picking out the key words for each one. If you have difficulty selecting the key words, think of facts, examples, reasons, and ideas that support your choices. This should help you pinpoint the key words. Study the example and subtract ideas that do not support the key words in the controlling idea. What ideas could be added?

Example:	Visitors to the forest can see and smell the refreshing signs of spring.

1. blue jay sitting on a branch of an oak tree
2. dandelions blooming in the meadow
3. water rushing down a brook
4. a pile of cow manure casting a "fragrant" aroma
5. snapping turtle sunning itself on a rock
6. rabbits scurrying into a bush
7. a gaggle of geese honking overhead
8. merry children tobogganing down a hillside

Which ideas did you subtract? Hopefully you subtracted 4, 7, and 8 because they violated the key words of *see*, *smell*, *refreshing*, and *spring*, leaving you with only five items on your list. You may feel five is not enough to write a complete paper. You can always think of more details that support the words *see* and *smell*.

You can also rewrite the controlling idea/topic sentence to expand its limits. By changing the key words *see* and *smell* to *sense*, you can open up your list to all the senses. Now item 7 could be used, and you can think of a lot more sensory ideas. (The "cow pie" in #4 will probably never be thought of as refreshing.)

SELECTING TOPICS AND KEY WORDS

EXERCISE 2: Select the topic and key words in each of the following student controlling ideas. Make a list of details to support each key idea. Complete the first two as a group activity. You might complete the others in groups.

1. A visit to historic Washington, D. C. enables tourists to reflect on many great men and women and their deeds in America's past.

2. The American consumer must sustain a bombardment of endless advertisements.

3. Quite often people become too involved in the hustle and bustle of everyday living.

4. The friendly sounds of West Valley High School's cafeteria become more recognizable as the days go by.

5. Educated feet are necessary for a good soccer fullback.

6. Gardening provides a source of relaxation for retired people.

POORLY WRITTEN CONTROLLING IDEAS

General statements and direct statements of fact do not make good controlling ideas. They are either much too general and vague, or they are "so what" type statements which need no support.

Example: Automobiles are useful.

This controlling idea/topic sentence is vague because it includes all automobiles and all the possible uses that can be made of them. This topic could probably never be exhausted.

Rewritten: Carpooling is a means of conserving fuel, money, and wear and tear on automobiles.

Note that the **topic** now is limited to carpooling, which in turn is limited to conserving fuel, money, and maintenance. The **key words** set a particular direction and organization. This topic sentence is much more specific than the first one. It could be limited even more by writing about just one of the suggested aspects.

Example: Spaghetti and meatballs are served in Italian ristorantes.

Because this is a pure direct statement of fact, you probably said, "So what," or "I know that." To improve this "So what" controlling idea, the writer made this statement specific by limiting the topic to a particular individual's way of preparing spaghetti and meatballs.

Rewritten: A non-Italian can learn how to make spaghetti and meatballs, a la Italian ristorante, by following Dominic Grassi's simple and yet delicious family recipe.

EXERCISE 3: The following controlling ideas/topic sentences are vague and unprovable. As a class, discuss what is wrong with each of them.

1. Girls appreciate many things.
2. In a typical spring day there is plenty of rain.
3. The new television season provides many new shows.
4. Men are better cooks than women.
5. Schools give too much homework.
6. Weather can cause problems for many people.
7. Everyone likes summer vacations during the summer.
8. All foreign made cars are cheaper than American made cars.

WRITING CONTROLLING IDEAS

Now would be a good time to practice writing your own controlling ideas. However, before you begin this activity, study the list of supportive ideas a high school girl chose after she brainstormed her topic on sightseeing in Chicago.

Since a well-written composition must be similar to a perfect circle with every idea contributing to the unity of the paper, the circle illustration shows how the details support the key words.

Controlling Idea: Chicago offers the sightseeing visitor a variety of treats.

> **Topic:** Chicago
> **Key Words:** offers, sightseeing visitor, variety of treats

Notice how each spoke of the circle supports the key words in the controlling idea. In order for a composition to be unified, each supportive idea must relate back and prove the key words. If, for instance, one of the spokes read *garbage-lined alleys*, this statement would have to be subtracted because it does not support the key words in the controlling idea, even though Chicago has many *garbage-lined alleys*.

Chicago! Chicago!

1. Chicago offers the sightseeing visitor a variety of treats.

2. Set on the blue, gray, shining, sometimes stormy waters of Lake Michigan, Chicago is clearly a water city. **3.** Twenty-two miles of beaches tie the city to the lake and on a summer day bring hundreds of thousands to the water's edge. **4.** Parks rim the shore like the setting of a jewel. **5.** The towering Sears Tower and the spiraling Marina City add interest to Chicago's already impressive skyline which contains eight out of the twelve tallest buildings in the world. **6.** New construction dots nearly every Loop block. **7.** Reading the signs of stores and factories seems something like paging through a mail order catalog cover to cover. **8.** Chicago, bold, brash, beautiful, with her dynamic businesses and industries, her tremendous resources, and her capacity for growth, presents a brilliant spectacle to the visitor.

EXERCISE 4: In the following exercise, decide which brainstormed items are related to each other. Then write a controlling idea which states the topic and the key words. Do these as a group activity.

1. **Topic: My cat, "Mittens"**
   --often carries candy wrappers around in her mouth
   --sleeps curled up in a paper bag
   --fights with a neighbor's cat
   --unrolls the bathroom toilet paper
   --crunches mice
   --chases dangling bathrobe belts
   --at night growls at her shadow in the window
   --got her leg mangled by a dog
   --neighbors have a funny cat
   --scratches on closed doors at night
   --sharpens her paws on good furniture

2. **Topic: Camping trip**
   --ocean too rough for swimming
   --rain all the time
   --tent leaked
   --lake biggest ever seen
   --bears stole hot dogs and hamburgers
   --camp stove wouldn't start
   --vacationed with neighbors
   --beautiful sunset last day
   --sister twisted ankle
   --sit in car during rain

3. **Topic: No homework over holidays**
   --too hard to remember
   --interferes with family activities
   --need a break from studying
   --easy to misplace
   --makes you upset with the teacher
   --got an "A" on same assignment last year
   --teacher will have to correct assignments when classes resume
   --lose assignment
   --never do it anyway

GENERAL TO SPECIFIC

One way of creating more specific controlling ideas is to funnel general topics to more specific subjects and then to include key words that limit the topic and give direction for the paper's organization.

Study the following examples to see how a general topic can be broken down into a specific topic. One way this can be accomplished is by using the journalistic questions and constantly narrowing the topic to make it more specific.

Example:

General Word	What?	shopping
Specific Place	Where?	Sears
Specific Type	What Kind?	back-to-school
Specific Time	When?	beginning of school
Specific Happening	What?	sound of fire alarm
Specific Mood	What?	panic and confusion

After all the specific ideas were listed, the students used the manipulatory skills from **Unit 2** to write a tentative controlling idea. Then they rearranged it to capture the reader's attention. This is the finished controlling idea:

Controlling Idea: Panic reigns in Sears as the fire alarm sends back-to-school shoppers into a state of confusion.

Look for the key words that lend themselves to list-making, e.g., **panic** and **confusion**. Knowing these words will help you expand and provide supportive ideas for the controlling idea.

Example:

General Word	What?	Olympics
Specific Sport	What?	Track and field
Specific Event	What?	Decathlon
Specific Skill	What about It?	requires greatest amount of athletic ability

Using the manipulatory skills, a group of high school students wrote the following controlling idea:

Controlling Idea: Of the Olympics' track and field events, the decathlon requires the greatest amount of athletic ability.

Special Hint: Most of the students thought the *Olympics'* controlling idea was excellent and would make an easy writing assignment. However, when asked to list the ten events of the decathlon, they could only name three or four events. Lesson learned:

When given freedom of choice in selecting a topic, make sure that you have personal knowledge or experience with the topic in order to have enough to write about.

EXERCISE 5: Narrow down the following general topics into specific ideas by using the journalistic questions. Then write a controlling idea by using the sentence manipulatory skills. Complete the first few as a group activity.

After you have written several of these general topics into specific controlling ideas, read some to a small group audience. See if their interest is captured and if they can pick out your topic and key words.

1. school spirit	10. television programs	19. horror movies
2. health	11. restaurants	20. rock groups
3. family traditions	12. pets	21. jobs
4. girlfriends	13. slumping team	22. allowances
5. clothing	14. teachers	23. arguments
6. parties	15. hobbies	24. weather
7. catching a mouse	16. nursing	25. history class
8. typing	17. hair styles	26. politics
9. athletics	18. computers	27. Sunday brunch

FINAL NOTE

In the different organizational patterns that follow, you will be taught how to write the controlling idea either as an implied control or as a topic sentence. One thing you should never do is to insult your audience by saying, "I will discuss . . ." or "I'm going to tell about." When you say things like that, what you are really saying is "Hey, I know you'll never figure this out, so I'd better tell you what I going to write about."

CONCRETE VERBS

One of the main purposes in writing is to communicate what is crystal clear in your mind to the mind of your reader. Concrete verbs enable your audience to share in your thoughts.

To make your sentences come alive, you must learn to recognize and then change weak verbs. One way to do this is to substitute more specific verbs for general ones.

The verbs *be, have, do* and *get* are the basic predicates in the English language. All other verbs are a more specified form of these words.

Here is a list of forms of the verbs *to be*, *to do*, *to have*, and *to get*.

To Be:	am, is, are, was, were, has been, had been, will be, will have been, being
To Do:	do, did, done, does
To Have:	have, has, had
To Get	get, gets, got

To Be

For example, look at the sentence, *Sylvester is happy.* Instead of using the verb *is*, be more specific. Think of the subject, *Sylvester*, and what he actually does to show his happiness. Try *Sylvester jumps for joy*.

To Have

When you substitute for the principal parts of the verb *to have,* use an action word that describes what the subject is doing. For example, the sentence *Sheila has a strong arm* can be rewritten *Sheila throws hard.*

To Do

When you substitute for forms of the verb *to do*, the noun can become the verb. *Rudy does his laundry in the wash tub* can be rewritten *Rudy washed his laundry in the wash tub* or *Rudy laundered his wash in the tub*. **To do the wash** becomes either **to wash the laundry** or **to launder**.

To Get

Finally, one other word that causes problems for writers is the word *gots*. When you were a child, you may have said, *I gots a big owie on my finner,* and everyone thought it was cute. But, as you grew up, you learned to pronounce *finger* correctly and to say *cut*, not *owie*. We just want to remind you that *gots* is no longer cute either, especially when you are writing. Instead of saying *Janey gots a lot of mashed potatoes*, you could say *Janey heaped a pile of mashed potatoes on her plate*. Thus, *to get* becomes *to heap*. Much better!

EXERCISE 1: Rewrite the following sentences substituting specific verbs for forms of *to be*, *to have*, *to do*, and *to get*. Also, expand each sentence to at least eight words. Do several of the sentences together in class as a warm-up. In fact, your teacher may encourage you to use a thesaurus to see who can come up with the most exciting action verbs.

Example: Emma **is** angry.
Rewritten: Slamming the door behind her, Emma **stomped** angrily home.

Example: The Super Bowl **is** over.
Rewritten: In a blaze of popping flashbulbs, the Super Bowl winners **hoisted** their coach high onto their shoulders.

1. The contest **was** over.
2. The movie **is** exciting.
3. The band concert **was** a flop.
4. Elmira **is** an unhappy child.
5. Calvin **had been** a story teller.
6. Donna **gots** a new dress.
7. Mrs. P. B. Jones **has** a new car.
8. The turkey **gots** a nice taste.
9. Fred **has** an analytical mind.
10. Bridget **does** well in biology.
11. Daryl **gots** a good job.
12. Gilberto **did** well at work.
13. Paul **did** the windows.
14. Ramona **did** a job on the boat.
15. Ryan and Eric **have** the measles.
16. The book **is** good.
17. Alfie **got** a light lunch.
18. I **got** an "F" in P. E.

EXACT VERBS

EXERCISE 2: Now that you understand the importance of writing with concrete verbs, select the *best* one for your purpose. Study the following sentences and determine the *best* verb for your desired impact. Select any word that is appropriate as long as you can defend your choice.

You will enjoy doing this activity as an oral exercise in class, or perhaps you would enjoy acting out your verb choices while members of the class try to name the word you have chosen.

1. Suddenly the Mercury Sable (died out, stopped, screeched to a halt), knocking down the stop sign.

2. The enraged lion (peered, glanced, glared) viciously at the trainer.

3. Carefreely Clem (trotted, strolled, skipped) down the boulevard.

4. As the marathon runner entered the homestretch, she (paced herself, sprinted, jogged) towards the finish line.

5. With a series of short jabs, the heavyweight champ (clobbered, belted, sprayed) his opponent.

6. Coyly Wendy (begged, charmed, enticed) her mother into giving her the keys to the Jeep Cherokee.

7. After being struck by lightning, the old oak tree (fell and bounced, shook and dropped, toppled and tottered) across the rutted road.

8. The mangy, ancient grizzly (staggered and stumbled, weaved and bobbed, ambled and shuffled) through the leaves covering the forest floor.

9. The fire was (snapping, blazing, burning) when Engine Company Two arrived on the scene.

10. When clumsy Stacey Burns dropped the pitcher of lemonade, it (splattered, shattered, splintered) all over the kitchen floor.

ACTIVE VOICE AND PASSIVE VOICE IN SENTENCES

When the subject of a sentence performs the action expressed, the verb is in the active voice. When the subject receives the action of the verb, the verb is in the passive voice.

Since the *subject-verb-object* sentence pattern is the type most frequently used in English, active voice sentences are more common than passive voice ones. Here are some examples:

Active Voice: Megan **cleaned** her room before her mom came home.
Passive Voice: The room **was cleaned** by Megan before her mom came home.

Active Voice: Duane scored the winning touchdown with one second to go.
Passive Voice: The winning touchdown was scored by Duane with one second to go.

The passive voice is formed by using the past participle and some form of the verb *to be: is, are, was, were, been,* etc.

- The new mall **will be built** at the La Grange Avenue exit.
- The game **was won** by the Bulls in the last second.

The choice of whether you use active or passive voice depends upon your purpose in the sentence. As a rule, however, active voice provides more force, is more direct, requires less words, relies less on forms of *to be,* and sometimes is easier to understand.

Example: A good chef **spends** many hours practicing his recipes.
                                (Active)

This sentence is much more forceful and direct than:

Revised: Many hours **will be spent** by a good chef practicing his recipes.
                                (Passive)

In the preceding active voice example, the subject is active and performs the action. Just listening to both of these sentences should tell you that the active voice sentence is more forceful.

You still have the option of using passive voice, of course. And it should be used under the following conditions:

1. The object or receiver of the action is more important than the doer.

    Our school choir **has been invited** to sing at the inauguration.

2. The writer wishes to emphasize the receiver of the action more than the doer.

    The senator **was asked** to resign because of his unethical practices.

3. The doer is not known.

    Not much food **was left** in the refrigerator.

As a general rule, use active voice more than passive voice.

EXERCISE 3: Rewrite the following sentences, changing active voice to passive voice, or passive voice to active voice. Add any necessary words.

1. Uncle Tunis teased Melissa about her black eye.
2. Karen and Jim are washing the family car before they sell it.
3. The surprise upset the Gibbons family.
4. Mexican bullfights are preceded by the colorful march of fighters in the arena.
5. Ichabod Crane was being pursued by the ghastly headless horseman.
6. Moe was catapulted into stardom by her picture appearing in the catalog.
7. Jim Harbaugh intentionally threw the ball out of bounds.
8. A special Slovak Christmas Eve dinner was being cooked by Aunt Josie.
9. Joey gave Mona a pearl necklace for her birthday.
10. Little Joey Petrik was given a standing ovation by the huge crowd.

SUMMARY

Using active, specific verbs is one of the keys to good writing. Strong verbs make your writing come alive for your audience. They breathe life into your sentences.

The third column of the **Sentence Opening Sheet** should help you identify verbs. Remember the **He** or **She**____tip if you have difficulty identifying verbs. See page 14.

Since all the writing assignments in *Stack* should flow from your own experiences, probably a natural paper to start with is the **Problem-Solving** paper. Everyone has experienced many problems in life and has worked through at least some of them to satisfying solutions. One of these problems could be the topic for this assignment.

STAGE ONE: PREWRITING

STUDENT LEARNING OBJECTIVES

1. The student will state a specific problem in the controlling idea.
2. The student will explain how the problem was solved.
3. The student will provide specific details with each attempt.
4. The student will use transition words to link ideas.
5. The student will write the paper in the first person point of view.
6. The student will use concrete verbs and will keep all verbs in the past tense.
7. The student will end the paper with a sense of finality.

WRITING PROMPT

Did you ever lose your little brother or sister in a shopping center? Did you ever get on the wrong bus and end up in the wrong part of town? Did you ever have to locate a friend living in an unfamiliar city? Did you ever have to talk your way out of a punishment? Did you ever try to convince your parents to increase your allowance so that you had enough money to buy a gift for someone special? Perhaps, you have experienced one of these or a similar problem for which you were able to figure out a solution.

One of the most important steps in the prewriting stage is brainstorming. With the class, brainstorm problems which you may have faced at some time in your life.

Just to help you get started with your brainstorming, take turns reading and discussing the topics listed on the next page.

PERSONAL PROBLEM TOPICS

1. Have you ever tried to get into an "R" rated movie without your parents?
2. Have you ever tried to get out of visiting Great-aunt Hildegarde because you hate her sloppy kisses, and you hate sitting like a Barbie doll for hours?
3. Have you ever tried to hide something from your parents? a bad report card? a broken vase? a stray kitten?
4. Have you ever tried to get your brother or sister to do a favor for you? the dishes? your homework? loan you money?
5. Have you ever tried to ditch someone you didn't want along?
6. Have you ever tried to avoid the school bully? a neighborhood dog? a local gang?
7. Have you ever tried to do well in school while holding a part-time job?
8. Have you ever tried to quiet down three screaming children while you were babysitting?
9. Have you ever tried to tell someone that you did not want to go out with him without hurting his feelings?

WRITING ACROSS THE CURRICULUM PROBLEM TOPICS

1. Have you ever had to write an explanation for an experiment in chemistry? in biology? in physics?
2. Have you tried to persuade a teacher to let you have longer to complete an assignment? or to give you a higher grade on a report? or not to give homework over the weekend?
3. Have you ever had to write a paper explaining how the Civil War began? or how wagon trains first started? or how the Egyptians influenced the world? or how the Great Wall of China was built?

The choice for the topic is **yours**.

THINK SHEET

A **Think Sheet** is the part of the prewriting stage where the writer thinks with pen in hand. It is the time to gather your thoughts into a list of ideas that may go into your first draft.

If you can make a list with very specific details about your topic, you will have **little trouble with the paper's content**. If you cannot make a list, you probably are trying to write a paper for which you do not have enough information. If this is the case, you will avoid frustrations by selecting a new subject.

It's okay to start over. You will have proved the usefulness of the **Think Sheet**. You discovered that you did not have enough information before you began writing a rough draft without sufficient details.

Before you fill out the **Think Sheet**, sit down and talk your subject through with a fellow student, a friend, a parent, Cousin Hattie, anybody you can get to listen. Talking it over will help you when you pick up that pen to write. This is a worthwhile prewriting activity.

After you complete your **Think Sheet**, show it to your teacher. She will tell you if you have enough material to begin writing. She might even ask you to share your **Think Sheet** with the class for group discussion. Or she may have you exchange your **Think Sheet** with a classmate.

EXERCISE 1: Before beginning work on your own **Think Sheet**, read the student model, **Detentions Solved**. With the class, answer these questions and be prepared to fill in a **Think Sheet** with your responses.

1. What type of background information did the writer include in the introductory paragraph?
2. What is the writer's problem as stated in the introductory paragraph?
3. What attempts were tried and failed?
4. Why did they fail? Do you know how the writer felt with each failed attempt?
5. Which attempt worked? Why did it work? How did the writer feel?
6. Are there any ideas that need to be expanded to be more specific? Where?
7. Did the writer use concrete verbs?
8. Are all the verbs in the past tense?
9. Are any sentences too wordy? In other words, does the writer need to subtract empty words?
10. What type of ending did the writer use?

Detentions Solved

1. At the beginning of my freshman year in high school, I ran into many difficulties such as opening my locker, finding the books I needed, finishing my many assignments on time. **2.** Pretty soon all of these problems worked themselves out in some way or another except for one in particular. **3.** I could never figure out how to get to my classes on time. **4.** This seems like a problem any simpleton could find the solution to, but with two thousand students jammed into the hallways and McAuley High School being so large, walking fifteen feet can take two minutes.

5. During the second week of school, I undoubtedly decided that I would find the answer to my impossible problem if it took me all of freshman year to do so. **6.** During the first period study hall while studying French, my first idea came to me. **7.** I just had to carry around with me more of my books, therefore, cutting down on trips to my locker in the English Hall. **8.** Setting my theory to the test shortly after lunch the same day, I carried all of the books needed for biology, history, algebra, and beginning strings. **9.** It resulted in total disaster. **10.** Either I dropped something or I could barely lift the overwhelming tower of books that slowed me down horribly.

10. After this incident, one might give up and just live with numerous after school and lunch detentions. **11.** Undaunted by that minor and insignificant setback, I set out to find another answer. **12.** The next day another idea came to me, only this time during French class instead of study hall. **13.** Seemed so logical--put simply, I would walk faster. **14.** Like the first attempt, this plan was put into effect soon after my third period lunch by my walking as fast as my legs would carry me. **15.** Unfortunately, I couldn't go very far. **16.** Receiving countless dirty looks, I accidentally bumped into numerous people; a few unknown foes formed quickly. **17.** As quickly as the hallways filled, the crowds thinned out. **18.** Quickening my pace to practically a sprint, I was commanded by an unfamiliar teacher to stop running and to walk in a civilized fashion. **19.** Arriving at algebra a full minute after the bell, a lunch detention slip waited for me on my desk.

20. The next day I mulled over my dilemma while riding the bus to school. **21.** As if a light bulb went on inside my head, I realized the only solution--walking outside! **22.** At first, doubts came to mind. **23.** What if I got to the door and the hallway had already cleared? **24.** How would I get back in? **25.** On a chance, I walked outside, and it worked. **26.** I walked outside to French class. **27.** Strolling into French with a look of triumph on my face, I glanced at the clock on the wall and smirked; I arrived at class with two minutes to spare. **28.** With an amused and bewildered look on my teacher's face, she said, "I see we're on time today, Mademoiselle Marquardt. To what do we owe this great pleasure?"

29. Smiling ever more triumphantly, I leaned back on my chair and opened my book. **30.** Walking outside provided a shorter walking distance and was less crowded.

31. Now I get to my classes with time to spare and never worry about getting a detention for tardiness again. **32.** Now that I solved my tardiness problem for this semester, will the same difficulty occur again the next semester when my classes change?

This student model was written by Jennifer Marquardt from Chicago, Illinois. Her high school has a sidewalk that runs parallel to the school buildings.

Name_____

Problem-Solving Think Sheet

1. Writer's Purpose_____

2. Background Information_____

_____

3. Specific Problem_____

4. Tentative Controlling Idea_____

_____

5. First Attempt and Why It Failed_____

_____

_____

6. Second Attempt and Why It Failed_____

_____

_____

7. Any Other Failed Attempt and Why It Failed_____

_____

_____

8. Attempt That Solved Problem and How It Worked_____

_____

Special Hint: If you cannot fill out this **Think Sheet** in detail, you probably do not know enough about the topic you have selected. Now is the time to discard your **Think Sheet** and begin again.

CONTROLLING IDEA

Your controlling idea should state the problem, and the key words should zero in on the specific nature of your difficulty. A well-written controlling idea will help you keep your *focus* throughout the paper.

You have two options in beginning this paper. First, you may reveal the problem immediately. In this way your audience never has to guess what you are writing about. They know from the beginning what your difficulty is.

Second, you may write an introductory paragraph which leads up to the problem by giving some background information about the problem and then incorporating the controlling idea in the last sentence of the paragraph.

The introductory paragraph should accomplish two important things. First, it must catch the attention of the reader by peaking his interest in your topic. Second, it must reveal your problem.

Model Introductory Paragraph

I should have listened to my older sister Ginger's advice. She had warned me not to accept Mrs. Palermo's offer of babysitting for the terror of 137th Street, the non-stop, human dynamo, little Ben Palermo. However, I thought I could handle anything. **Little did I know that trying to put two-year-old Ben to sleep would cause me to age ten years in a few short hours.**

ORGANIZING THE PAPER

Organize your ideas in a chronological (time) sequence. Include at least two attempts which you tried that failed and tell why they failed and how you felt. Then you must tell the attempt that worked and explain how it worked.

With each attempt use journalistic questions to support your controlling idea. Explain **who** was involved, **what** you tried, **where** and **when** it took place, **why** it failed, and **how** you felt.

If you are writing a multi-paragraph paper, you will need to write a paragraph about each attempt you tried. Write one paragraph for each attempt. Your first attempted solution and explanation of why it failed will be the first paragraph of the body of your paper. Your second attempted solution and explanation of why it failed will be the second paragraph and so on.

POINT OF VIEW

Since you are writing about a personal problem, write this paper in the first person point of view. Avoid *you*.

Here is a list of first person personal pronouns:

I, me, my, mine, we, us, our, ours

GLUING TOGETHER IDEAS

In writing your first draft, be sure that all of your ideas are linked so that the reader knows when one attempt ends and another begins.

In this paper you should use transitions words that indicate a shift of ideas. Here is a brief list of appropriate transition words for organizing your work:

first, second, third, finally, thus, next,
now, then, furthermore, later in the day,
in addition, while, gradually, etc.

ENDING

You must be careful that your paper does not stop abruptly but ends naturally. (Please avoid using *The End*. This insults your reader. He can tell that it is *the end*.)

For this paper your ending may either be the logical solution or the frustrations you experienced because the problem could not be solved. Or perhaps the ending may come as a surprise because of the way you presented your alternate attempts.

If you are writing a multi-paragraph composition, you might summarize your solutions or write some final commentary on what you learned. No matter what ending you decide upon, make sure that it is part of your overall planning and leaves the reader with the impression that your composition is over.

STAGE TWO: WRITING THE FIRST DRAFT

With your **Think Sheet** in front of you, write your first draft. Number each sentence and skip lines. This will make it easier for your proofreading partner to criticize your paper in the rewriting stage.

Also, do not worry about mechanical errors at this time. It is much more important that you write down your ideas without pausing to correct every mistake. That's what the rewriting stage is for.

Here are some short-term goals to consider as you write your first draft:

1. You need to state your **specific problem** in the beginning of the composition.
2. You need to **organize** your ideas in a chronological sequence.
3. Each attempt must include **specific details**. Let your reader know how you felt when each attempt failed.
4. Use **transition words** to show the shift of ideas.
5. Write this paper in **first person point of view:** I, *we, us, our, my, mine*. Do not shift reference to *you know*.
6. Since this paper is about a problem you have already solved, keep all the verbs in the **past tense**.
7. Your **ending** should leave your reader with a sense of finality.
8. If your paper contains dialogue, note the punctuation rules on pages 181-182.

Now write your first draft.

STAGE THREE: REWRITING

SENTENCE OPENING SHEET

After you have written your first draft, fill out the special **Sentence Opening Sheet**. Your SOS should include the following information:

1. First four words of each sentence.
2. Transitions to indicate a shift from one attempt to the next.
3. *You* words.
4. Past tense verbs.
5. Number of words per sentence.

Here are the **symbols** to put above each column on the SOS Sheet.

Var	Frag	"You'" Glue	VT VP	RO VAR
First Four Words Per Sentence		**Special**	**Verbs**	**# of Words**

As you examine your completed **Sentence Opening Sheet**, ask yourself these questions about each column:

Column One   **First Four Words of Each Sentence**

1. Do all of my sentences begin with the same openings, e. g., *I, The, And, then,* etc.?
2. Can I combine and/or rearrange some of the sentences to make them more interesting?
3. Do any of my sentences begin with subordinating conjunctions (glue words)? Are these sentence fragments? (Remember the *I BELIEVE THAT* tip.)

Column Two   **Special (Teacher Pet Peeve Column)**

1. Did I use transition words to shift from one attempt to the next?
2. Did I use *you know*, thereby shifting reference to second person?

Column Three   **Verbs**

1. Are all of my verbs in the past tense?
2. Did I repeat the same weak verbs over and over again?
3. Could I make my sentences more interesting by using concrete verbs?

Column Four   **Number of Words Per Sentence**

1. Are any of my overly long sentences run-ons?
2. Can I combine some short, choppy sentences to make them more interesting?
3. Did I use short sentences to stress an idea?

PEER EVALUATION USING A CHECKLIST SHEET

When you critique your partner's **Problem-Solving** paper, you will be reading a paper dealing with the same composition assignment you had to write. In checking over his paper, ask yourself if the writer considered you when he wrote the paper or did he short-circuit you and make huge assumptions.

If your partner's paper seems unclear and full of gaps (missing information), he probably assumed that you knew more about his problem than you really did. Sometimes it is easier to spot mistakes on someone else's paper than your own. Treat his paper as if it were your own.

EXERCISE 2: Before exchanging papers and revising your first draft, critique **The New Bike** model as a class activity. Use either the **SOES Sheet (grading sheet)** or the **Checklist Sheet** as your guide.

The New Bike

1. I fell off my bike when I was small. **2. The problem** was that I wasn't used to it because it was new.

3. First, I got some training wheels to help me stay up but they was loose and "plunk" down I went.

4. Secondly, I had somebody hold the bike while I pedal but that didn't work either because the person would get tried and then I would fall. **5. I would** go a little bit and then I would fall.

6. **I was** just about to give up when I said to myself, "try it once more, dummy, so I try it. **7. I went** quite a distance without falling. **8. When I** try it again I didn't.

9. This was the beginning of my riding a bike.

10. Now I can ride a bike real well and faster. **11. When I** remember how hard it was for me when I was small I said to myself, "now why didn't I do this in the first place?" **12. And that** was the end of my experience with the new bike. **13.** THE END!

Writer's Name_____

Corrector's Name_____

Problem-Solving Checklist Sheet

1. What is the writer's specific problem as stated in the beginning of the composition? (If you do not know what the problem is, it is not clearly stated.)

2. Is each failed attempt specific, or does the writer need to expand by adding more concrete details? Where?

3 . Does the attempt that *worked* need to be expanded? If so, provide the writer with some ideas.

4. Which transition words does the writer use to indicate the shift from one attempt to the next?

5. Does the writer end on a sense of finality? Does the writer include the word *end* in his last sentence?

6. Are all the verbs in the past tense? Which verbs did you like?

7. Does the writer shift his point of view from first person to second person to third person?

8. Does the writer need to combine and/or rearrange any sentences to avoid repetitious sentence openings, e.g., *I, The, And then,* etc.?

9. What one suggestion could you give the writer to help him improve his **Problem-Solving** paper?

SUPPLEMENTAL EXERCISE (Run-Ons and Fragments)

Run-On Tip

A run-on sentence is two or more sentences written as though they were one sentence. The writer does **not** punctuate correctly.

Example: I attempted to con her into letting me go she didn't agree to my pleas.

Here are four ways to correct run-on sentences:

1. Use a period as an end punctuation. Capitalize the first word of the second sentence.

    I attempted to con her into letting me **go. She** didn't agree to my pleas.

2. Use a comma plus a coordinator (**BOYS FAN = but, or, yet, so, for, and**, and **nor**).

    I attempted to con her into letting me **go, but** she didn't agree to my pleas.

3. Use a semicolon if the two sentences are closely related in meaning.

    I attempted to con her into letting me **go; she** didn't agree to my pleas.

4. Rewrite the sentence using subordinating conjunctions (glue words), relative pronouns (WH words), and present participles or gerunds (ING words).

    Although I attempted to con her into letting me **go, she** didn't agree to my pleas.

A good way to check for run-on sentences is to read your sentence *aloud* to hear for the natural "pause." If there is a pause, check for proper punctuation.

Example:　Homer complained about his grade in English he forgot that he failed to turn in his homework for the last six weeks.

In reading this sentence aloud, do you hear the pause between *English* and *he*? Run-on. Rewrite the sentence in the correct way.

Fragment Tips

A fragment is a group of words that does not express a complete thought.

A good way to check for fragments in a paragraph is to read the paragraph backwards one sentence at a time. You begin with your *last* sentence and stop. Does it make sense? This reading aloud helps you to hear incomplete thoughts.

Example: Frenchie Mahoney skated towards the goal. Controlling the puck with the skill of the Great Gretzky.

Can you hear the fragment? *Controlling the puck with the skill of the Great Gretzky.*

Revised: Controlling the puck with the skill of the Great Gretzky, Frenchie Mahoney skated towards the goal.

Remember, another way to check for fragments is to read the expression **I Believe That** right *before* the group of words you are checking. If the statement sounds confusing, it is probably a fragment.

Example: Because Kirk answered the call.

I Believe That because Kirk answered the call.

Fragment!

Certain words cause fragments: subordinating conjunctions (glue words), relative pronouns (WH words), and ING words (verbals). Look for these words if you think your group of words is a fragment.

Fragments:

Although Ellisa won the award.

Which won the game.

Singing in the shower.

EXERCISE 3: Identify and correct the run-on sentences and fragments in the following sentences. Also, look for verb tense inconsistency. All the verbs should be written in the past tense.

1. The first thing I tried was calling her up on the telephone she just kept hanging up on me.

2. I heard from some friends around school that she already had a date for the dance that's why she wouldn't go with me.

3. Now deciding which path to take. Of course, I take the wrong one the path led me back to the fork.

4. Mrs. Jacob went running in a state of panic just to buy her son a hair dryer, she walks out of Casey's Department Store, she headed for Sears.

5. Third, I gots all my books for my afternoon classes fled toward the line but I failed because the weight of the books slowed me down.

6. When we first noticed it. The inner tube was only a few feet away. I decided to go swim after it but soon enough I remembered I couldn't swim I started to sink.

7. We ran over to help she asked us to push the car as we tried to push the car we found that the brakes are jammed.

8. One Saturday morning I get on the plane to Los Angeles to visit my cousin. Which was a wonderful experience for my first time flying.

STAGE FOUR: PUBLISHING

Publishing provides the writer with an opportunity to share his **Problem-Solving** paper beyond the editing partner or cooperative learning group.

There are many forms of publishing. Since many of you probably delved into your past to select an exciting topic of interest, your teacher may have a few volunteers read their problem-solution paper to the entire class.

Another publishing activity is giving a speech. The organization would be the same as writing a composition:

• Peaking the listeners' interest with the introduction.

• Focusing on the problem and the attempts tried and failed.

• Arranging the details in a logical sequence.

• Supporting the ideas with details.

• Using appropriate language.

• Ending the speech in an interesting way.

Finally, you might want to select this piece for your writing portfolio.

Every language has a special word form for conveying the notion of motion. In English this form is the **ING** word.

Present participles are the ING forms of verbs which function as adjectives. Gerunds are ING forms of verbs working as nouns. You will be using ING words as adjectives and nouns instead of as verbs in your next writing assignment--**Describing Chronologically** paper.

One clue to remember is that ING words can only function as verbs if they have a helping verb (*is, are, was, were, has, been, have been, had been,* etc.).

BEGINNING SENTENCES WITH ING WORDS

EXERCISE 1: Subtract all forms of the helping verb **to be:** *is*, *are*, *was*, or *were*. In this way you will be using ING words as present participles and gerunds instead of verbs. Then use your **writer's vocabulary** skills and **combine** and **rearrange** the sentences. No fragments.

Example: The pouring rain **was pounding** against the crystal clear window. It smashed the glass.

Revised: **Pounding against the crystal clear window,** the pouring rain smashed the glass.
or
The pouring rain, **pounding against the crystal clear window,** smashed the glass.

Example: Ann Marie **was shooting** the free throw. She won the championship game in overtime.

Revised: **Shooting the free throw**, Ann Marie won the championship game in overtime.

Punctuation Rule: When a sentence begins with an ING introduction (Participial Phrase), it needs a comma to set off the introductory phrase to keep the meaning clear.

1. The giant circus elephants **were amusing** all who saw them.
   They lumbered and clambered through the big top.

2. Rich Preng toed the pitching rubber.
   He **was taking** a sign from Timmy Braun.

3. Kathy **was toasting** the bread. She opened the jar.
   She **was spreading** the peanut butter on the sandwich.

4. Milton **was buckling** his armor.
   He grasped the spear.
   He bellowed mightily.
   He **was crawling** under the bed.

5. The fireman **was climbing** the ladder.
   He broke the window.
   He entered the smoke-filled building.

6. Blanche **was scribbling** in her medical notebook.
   She typed her notes.

7. Willie **was putting** on his vest.
   He sauntered over to the crap table.
   He lost his underwear.

8. The beggar **was pleading** for coffee money.
   He approached the well-dressed man.
   He humbly tipped his hat.

9. Cecil **was raising** his baton.
   He waited for silence.
   He directed the Quigley chorus.

10. Tyrone **was looking** at the typewriter.
    He eyed Rene and Sandy. He typed just one more sentence.

SENSE APPEALING WORD CLUSTERS

Since the next writing assignment is a descriptive composition, you should use as many sense appealing words as possible. Any word which does not directly appeal to your senses will be termed an *empty* word. The subtraction of empty words is a stylistic approach you can use in your writing.

EXERCISE 2: Rearrange the following word groups (fragments) by **subtracting** *empty* words. Make sure that you also subtract *is*, *are*, *was* and *were*. Write ING and ED endings without writing fragments. If necessary, **expand**.

Example: The clouds **which were** white **were** floating above and **were** specking the sky.

Revised: The floating, white clouds **specked** (verb) the sky.
    or
    The sky-**specking**, **floating** white clouds (expansion needed))
    sailed overhead.

Example: The sky **was** forming into a blanket **which was** stretching endlessly to the horizon.

Revised: **Stretching** endlessly to the horizon, the sky blanketed the earth.
    or
    The endlessly **stretching** sky blanketed the horizon.

1. A flash of lightning **which was** streaking across the sky **which was** shaking the ground.

2. The breeze **which was** slight **was** harshly rustling the leaves **which was** becoming a gale **which was** sweeping.

3. The thunder **which was** echoing **was** like a huge kettle drum **which was** reverberating.

4. The heavens **which were** erupting in a flash of light **which were** being followed by a peal of thunder **which was** rolling across the sky.

5. The grass **which was** lush and **which was** green **was** flowing in soft tufts **which were** spilling over the bank **which was** steep.

6. A tree **which was** oak and **which was** loitering in the sun during the midday **which was** warm.

7. Its leaves **which were** dark and green **which were** drooping listlessly.

8. The pond **which were** shimmering **which were** studded with sparks of sunlight **which were** reflecting the sky **which was** blue and **which was** pale.

9. The sun **which was** disappearing **which was** leaving the heavens **which were** swirling.

10. The children **who were** frolicking in the playgrounds and the cyclists **who were** pedaling along merrily.

SUMMARY

ING words are powerful tools in writing. They take ordinary ideas and make them extraordinary. Use them to make your ideas come alive for your audience.

- **Weaving** in and out of the mercilessly moving stream of traffic . . .

- **Careening** off the guard rails . . .

- **Spinning** down an icy stretch of I-57 . . .

- **Whipping** everything into a frenzy, a cold, cruel wind . . .

- The sun disappeared leaving the heavens a **swirling, striving** mass of storm and wrath.

To write a composition about a storm you will want to include ING words to indicate action, e. g., *the howling wind, the pouring rain*, or *the booming thunder in the distance*.

STAGE ONE: PREWRITING

STUDENT LEARNING OBJECTIVES

1. The student will make the storm the focus of the paper.
2. The student will organize the paper in the before, during, and after time sequences.
3. The student will balance the organization in the before, during, and after time sequences by repeating ideas in each sequence.
4. The student will use transitions to indicate a shift in the three time sequences.
5. The student will use ING words to convey the notion of action and motion.
6. The student will identify and correct ING word fragments.

WRITING PROMPT

The primary choice for your topic is a description of a storm. You should select a location that has a specific meaning for you, e. g., the beach, the forest, a city park, a neighborhood site, etc. In this way you will be familiar with the specific details associated with your location.

Select a specific type of storm that you experienced first hand. It could be a rain, sleet, wind, ice, or snow storm. A tornado, hurricane, or typhoon are other possibilities. Even an earthquake would be an appropriate topic. You also will be describing the time changes before, during, and after the occurrence.

Keep in mind that your purpose will be to describe the effects of the storm on the objects located in your site to an audience unfamiliar with the area.

ALTERNATE TOPICS

Since the main purpose is to describe the changes that take place in a specific location in three different time sequences, there are many alternate and writing across the curriculum topics which you might choose. Your topic could be any setting with a before, during, and after sequence.

1. The school locker room before/during/after an athletic event.
2. The school cafeteria before/during/after lunch time.
3. The school gym before/during/after the homecoming dance.
4. The science lab before/during/after an experiment.
5. The home economics room before/during/after cooking class.
6. The auto and/or wood shop before/during/after class.
7. The floor of the stock market before/during/after a trading session.
8. Main Street before/during/after the St. Patrick's Day Parade.
9. The starting line before/during/after the start of a marathon.
10. The site of an historical event before/during/after.

What are some other possible topics? Brainstorm.

THINK SHEET

A specific use of the **Think Sheet**, other than making a complete list, is to suggest a basic organization for your paper and provide a sense of balance to it.

Complete your own **Think Sheet** after studying the model **Think Sheet** and student paper. Use the following questions as a guide.

1. What is the specific locale for the storm?
2. What type of storm is described?
3. What are the objects/persons described?
4. Are all objects/persons described in the before, during, and after sections?
5. What are the ING action words used?
6. What transition words did the writer include?
7. Which verbs show action?
8. Are the verbs in the same tense?
9. Should any sentences be combined or rearranged?
10. How does the paper end?

NAME_____Steve Wagner_____

Describing Chronologically Think Sheet

1. What is the locale of the storm/event?_____Marblehead, MA_____

2. Fill out the storm/event grid using ING words to indicate motion and activity. Make the storm/event the central character. Avoid using people's names. Expand using the journalistic questions.

Object/Person	Before	During	After
1. sky	Off-gray, overcast	Blackened, frightened	Reddish, cloudless
2. Atlantic Ocean	Small waves, cold, mist-covered	Frightening high waves, rain-speckled	Calm, peaceful
3. Oceanside inhabitants	Working hard, sending danger	Calm, confident	Business as usual
4. Animal life	Sensing danger, preparing	Couldn't be seen	Looking for food
5. Tourists	Happy, normal	Scared; sheltered	Weary, thankful, shaken
6. Wind	Gusty, cool, dying down	Gale force—damaging	Calm, swirling gusts
7. Trees	Bending gently	Uprooted, swaying	Debris on ground
8. Temperature	Hot—except breeze	Cold, freezing	Cold--milder

Helpful Hint: In writing your first draft, combine the above ideas into sentences. Use ING words. Expand when necessary.

The Storm

1. Its bright rays **shining** through the cloudy sky, the hot sun gave the appearance of any other autumn day. **2.** The only relief found on this steamy afternoon seemed to be the cool gusts of wind **blowing** in off the mist-covered Atlantic.

3. On many autumn days such as this, one could see children **playing** in the Atlantic, but today the children as well as animal life took refuge in their homes, **sensing** a danger known only to the experienced. **4.** Oceanside residents, feverishly **working** to moor their boats to the docks, speckled the shoreline. **5. Looking** toward the northeast, one could see a band of clouds, black and ominous, **rolling** across the sky to further obscure the once visible sun. **6.** The waves, **coming** in off the Atlantic, grew in size and strength, while fish tried to avoid **hitting** the rocky shore. **7. Blowing** in faster and colder, the swirling wind formed minute whirlpools in the usually calm cove.

8. Now accompanied by rain, the storm's force became so **frightening** it made its onlookers stand in awe. **9.** Once **bending** to the light oceanside breezes, the trees along the shoreline now took the full, **devastating** force of the gale wind that had arisen. **10.** Waves, now **frighteningly** high, swallowed small **seafaring** vessels in single gulps. **11.** Because the sun remained obscured by storm clouds, the temperature dropped to the **freezing** point, **forcing** tourists to take refuge at any house that would have them. **12.** Many travelers could find no refuge at the hands of these seemingly confident yet obviously frightened ocean side dwellers, so they turned back to face the **devastating** storm.

13. After close to three hours of continuous downpour, the rain began to subside. **14.** Small **swirling** gusts of wind continued, yet the Atlantic appeared calm. **15.** The **setting** sun cast a beautiful orange color over the now cloudless sky, and nobody could spot any signs of the tremendous deluge that had occurred not one half hour ago. **16.** Throughout the skies soared gulls, **searching** for food that the mighty Atlantic had coughed up. **17.** In its wake the storm left chimneys broken, trees uprooted, and windows shattered. **18.** Debris of all kinds served as grim reminders of the storm and its deadly force.

19. As night came, the dwellers prepared for tomorrow as if nothing had happened. **20.** Tourists, shaken by the storm, continued on their way, thankful for their safety. **21.** Soon, the darkness of night fell on the little town of Marblehead, Massachusetts, calmly and peacefully, as it had done so many times before.

Describing Chronologically Think Sheet

1. What is the locale of the storm/event?_____

2. Fill out the storm/event grid using ING words to indicate motion and activity. Make the storm/event the central character. Avoid using people's names. Expand using the journalistic questions.

Object/Person	Before	During	After
1.			
2.			
3.			
4.			
5.			
6.			
7.			
8.			

Helpful Hint: In writing your first draft, combine the above ideas into sentences. Use ING words. Expand when necessary.

CONTROLLING IDEA

A composition does not always need a *stated* controlling idea. Instead, the writer can immediately plunge into the action of the story. For this paper you should immediately begin to describe the setting before the storm or before the major event takes place. Here is an example:

Suddenly Comes the Storm

Everything was warm and quiet. The lush, green grass flowed in soft tufts down the gentle knoll and spilled over the steep bank toward the mirror that was a pond. A stout, old oak loitered in the warm midday sun, its dark, green leaves drooping listlessly in the satisfying warmth, and the rich brown of its ancient trunk accentuating the green of the meadow. It was spring.

As you noted from the above example, the description of the opening scene before the storm took place served as the introductory paragraph for the composition.

ORGANIZING THE PAPER

This paper should be organized in a chronological sequence with before, during, and after descriptions of the objects that are part of the storm's location. Each time sequence must include the same five, six or seven objects or people which you have listed on your **Think Sheet**. Each object or person should be fully described using ING words whenever possible.

If you are having trouble describing each object or person, **expand** by asking yourself the journalistic questions: who? what? where? when? why? and how?

Example: Object: tree

                Question: **What** was the tree doing during the storm?

                Answer: sway**ing** in the violent breeze

GLUING TOGETHER IDEAS

In this paper you must use transition words that bridge ideas that otherwise might seem unrelated. Use words that indicate time.

In the sentences *The sun shone brightly in a clear, blue sky. Gathering storm clouds darkened the beach*, the ideas seem illogical because transition words are missing. However, by adding the expression *in a few minutes*, the sentences become related.

Here is an example of the two sentences being glued together:

The sun shone brightly in a clear, blue sky. **In a few minutes** gathering storm clouds darkened the beach.

> **Transition Words:** once, then, now, today, at length, soon, while, yesterday, late afternoon, early, at midday, finally, later, in a few minutes, suddenly, after a long time, etc.

EXERCISE 1: Add transition words to connect the following ideas.

1. Abraham Lincoln was born in Kentucky. He went to school in Illinois. He fought in the Black Hawk War. He was appointed postmaster in New Salem. He was elected the President of the United States in 1860.

2. The nurses complete the surgical preparation on the patient. The patient is placed on a surgical cart. He ascends in the elevator to the surgical floor. He is wheeled into the operating room. He remembers counting off, "One hundred, ninety-nine, ninety-eight, . . ."

TABOO WORDS

In writing your description, avoid overusing forms of *to be*: *is, are, was*, and *were*. Also, concentrate on concrete and specific verbs to describe the storm's/event's actions, eliminating such weak verbs as *got* and *gots*. Finally, since this paper is written in the third person point of view, avoid using second person pronouns: *you, your*, and *yours*.

ENDING

Your ending must not be abrupt. It must flow naturally out of the paper's development. For example, if the paper has the impact of fear on the reader, it would end with a sense of relief. If the people were enjoying themselves and frolicking before the storm, the paper might end with disappointment.

Whatever ending you decide upon, remember that the objects and persons described in the before and during sections of the storm must also be included in the ending section.

POINT OF VIEW

In your writing the **Problem-Solving** paper you used first person pronouns since you were the central character narrating a special problem. Since the storm or the event is the central character in this paper, you must describe from the third person viewpoint.

Even though you might be selecting a site where you personally experienced a storm, you must avoid making references to yourself. The purpose for this paper is to describe, not to narrate.

Third person viewpoint requires the use of third person pronouns such as: tree = it, parking lot attendant = he, little girl = she, mother's cry = her cry, baseball team = they, the birds' feathers = their, frightened youngsters = them.

STAGE TWO: WRITING THE FIRST DRAFT

With your **Think Sheet** in front of you, write your first draft without being concerned about making errors. In fact, feel free to use *is*, *are*, *was*, and *were* which will be identified on your **Sentence Opening Sheet**. Errors can be corrected when you write your final draft.

Remember that your composition should be written in past tense verbs since you are writing about a storm that has already occurred. Also, remember to skip lines and number your sentences. This will make it easier to revise your paper.

Now write your first draft.

STAGE THREE: REWRITING

SENTENCE OPENING SHEET

After you have written your first draft, fill out the **Sentence Opening Sheet** following the instructions you were given for the **Problem-Solving** paper. For the special column, in addition to transition words and *I* or *you*, you should list any ING words you have used. Your teacher may even want a third **Special** column for listing your sensory appeal words.

Be sure to check your paper for fragments caused by the use of ING words or WH words. Also, watch for run-ons or short, choppy sentences.

Also, note any helping verbs you may have used and look out for dull, repetitive verbs, e.g. "**began** to rain," "**started** to drizzle," instead of "rained" or "drizzled" which are better.

Remember that the **SOS Sheet** is a tool to help you decide how to revise your paper. The better use you make of it, the better your paper will turn out.

PEER EVALUATION USING A CHECKLIST

When you criticize your partner's **Describing Chronologically** paper, you will be reading a paper dealing with the same composition assignment you had to write. As you check over this paper, ask yourself if the writer considered you, the audience, when he wrote the paper. Did he guide you carefully by using transition words between objects/persons and the sequences, or did he make huge assumptions which left you guessing?

If he left you guessing in places, help him by showing him the gaps. Remember to treat his paper as if it were your own. He will appreciate your helping him to write a better paper.

Describing Chronologically Checklist Sheet

1. How does the writer maintain his focus on the topic throughout the composition?

2. Are there any items or objects that appear in each time sequence that are not fully developed? How could you expand them?

3. Which transition words did the writer use in each time sequence?

4. Indicate the ING words that show motion and activity by circling them on the first draft.

5. Check the ending of the paper. Make sure the writer included all the objects and persons in the *after* section of the paper.

6. Check the writer's verb choices. Make sure the writer didn't mistake participles for verbs. Check for ING fragments.

7. Circle *is*, *are*, *was*, and *were*. Put a check beside dull or repetitive verbs. Check to see that all the verbs are in past tense.

8. Which one suggestion would you make to your partner to improve his paper?

FINAL COPY AFTER PEER EVALUATION

Before submitting your final "neat" and error-free copy, follow the same procedure you used in revising your **Problem-Solving** paper. Make sure you reread your final draft aloud three or four times, each time concentrating on one specific objective: specific details, past tense verbs, third person point of view, etc.

As a final check, evaluate your final draft based on the student learning objectives as stated on page 59 of this unit and the **SOS** sheet. If you discover something that needs to be corrected, do it.

STAGE FOUR: PUBLISHING

One of the best ways of sharing these compositions is to do some oral reading. Students can volunteer to read their storm paper to the class, or they can read them in their cooperative learning groups.

Another activity would be to compile a booklet of the best description from the class. Or submit your composition for a special feature in your school's literary magazine. You might want to include a drawing or a photo of your location.

Finally, you might select your description for your writing portfolio.

Up to this point you have learned to **combine** and **rearrange** sentences into larger and more complicated sentences with the purpose of writing a variety of sentence patterns. You achieved this by using subordinating conjunctions (glue words) and relative pronouns (WH words) to combine ideas.

The group of words that is most important to you should always be the part of the sentence that can stand by itself. The group of lesser importance should be introduced by a subordinating conjunction or relative pronoun and combined with the sentence of greater importance. This is called **subordination**.

EXERCISE 1: Combine the following sentences using subordinating conjunctions (glue words). First determine which idea has the greater importance and then place a glue word before the lesser idea. Next **rearrange** the glue word to shift impact. Do the first two as a group activity.

Example: **Nathan Andrew was severely punished** because he broke the window.

The sentence of greater importance is *Nathan Andrew was severely punished* because it is the part of the sentence which will stand by itself. The subordinating conjunction (glue word) *because* introduces the idea of lesser importance, *because he broke the window.*

If you want to stress the idea that *Nathan Andrew broke the window*, **rearrange** the sentence and put the subordinating conjunction before the lesser idea as follows:

Example: **Nathan Andrew broke the window** because he was severely punished.

SUBORDINATING CONJUNCTIONS (Glue Words):
after, although, as, as if, as long as, as though, because,
before, if, in order that, even though, since, though, unless,
until, when, where, while, whenever, wherever, etc.

1. The fighting Titans had lost seven games in a row.
   Coach Karen Hansen expressed confidence in her young players.

2. Carman was eating at Timmy's Diner.
   A semi-truck smashed through the picture window.

3. The movie starlet stepped out of the door.
   Swarms of admirers gasped at her every move.

4. She took it.
   Leta found an opportunity.

5. Tom trudged painfully through the snow.
   He had a broken leg.

6. A hush fell over the expectant audience.
   Maestro O'Gallagher ascended the podium.

7. Ms. Nancy Wrench wanted the matter settled.
   She attended the truck drivers' meeting.

8. The dancers swirled quickly.
   It made Iris dizzy.

9. The upset teachers may strike in September.
   They want their contract demands met.

10. You scratch my back.
    I'll scratch your back.

Punctuation Rule: Remember, **whenever** a sentence begins with a subordinate clause, it must have a comma to set off the introduction. (Notice the **whenever**.)

SUBORDINATING CONJUNCTION FRAGMENTS

Subordinating conjunctions are used to show the relationship between ideas. They are used to connect ideas that are not equally important. The clause that begins with the subordinating conjunction is dependent on the main clause for its meaning. By itself this glue word clause is a fragment.

Examples:

- **After** Curtis had prepared the gyros plate for Helen.
- **As** Rod Stewart walked onto the stage.
- **When** the defensive tackle lumbers onto the field.
- **Even though** Melanie looked great in her cashmere coat.

71

Incomplete sentences are more of a problem in writing than in speech. If you say an incomplete thought, a fragment, while you are speaking, your listener can interrupt to ask you for clarification or can infer what you meant.

Many students write fragments because their minds work faster than they are able to write. Physically they are finishing sentence number one. While their minds are on sentence number two. OOPS. That's a fragment. Right?

A good way to practice hearing fragments is to reread a composition ***backwards*** one sentence at a time, stopping after each "sentence" and seeing if it makes sense. See if you can identify the fragment here:

> The old hermit stayed in his mountainside cabin. Until the first snow of the fall.

Also, remember the **I BELIEVE THAT** tip. Try it.

> **I BELIEVE THAT** until the first snowfall of the fall.

Is that a fragment?

EXERCISE 2: The following word groupings begin with subordinating conjunctions. Correct each fragment by **expanding** with your own words. Be imaginative. After writing each sentence once, **rearrange** it a second time so that each opening does not begin with a subordinating conjunction.

Example: Since we all love pork hocks and sauerkraut.

Sentence: Since we all love pork hocks and sauerkraut, **my mom prepares this meal every Sunday afternoon for our family dinner.**

1. If Mr. Bonk would leave me alone for a few minutes.
2. After Ferdinand passed his driving test.
3. Although Jose's surprise party began at 7:30 P.M.
4. As Carina strolled along the seashore.
5. After Ms. Erin Jane Bobb won the Miss Alabama Teenage Pageant.
6. Because Stuart Alan has such an enthusiastic personality.
7. Even though we did not receive any homework over the weekend.
8. Whenever Myles finishes his experiment in science class.
9. Since Dwight and Leigh had to go home in separate cars.
10. When Yan Soo stood up to take her food tray back to the kitchen.

RELATIVE PRONOUNS (WH WORDS)

Another way of combining a sentence of greater importance with one of lesser importance is to begin the sentence of lesser importance with a relative pronoun (WH word). Relative pronouns are most often used with word groupings placed in the middle of a sentence.

> **RELATIVE PRONOUNS:** who, whom, whose, which, what, and *that.
> * (There's always an exception to the rule!)

Sometimes a type of sentence fragment results from relative pronouns used incorrectly. The writer leaves the sentence hanging by chopping off a main idea or leaving the relative pronoun clause stand by itself.

> The man who fell down the stairs.

EXERCISE 3: Correct the relative pronoun (WH word) fragments in the following sentences by expanding and/or combining and rearranging. First, listen to the following sentences and discuss what is missing in each of them. Write the corrected sentences on a separate sheet of paper.

- The little baby **who is always playing in the crib.**

- The small tremors disturbed the Ramsey household. **Which were caused by the earthquake.**

- The old suit **which sat in the corner of the closet.**

WH word fragments can be corrected by expanding or combining and/or rearranging.

> The little baby **who is always playing in the crib** loves throwing his rattle at Babe, the family dog. **(Expanding)**

1. The student who enjoys reading.

2. The new television show which was highly praised by the critics from the public television network.

3. The 1921 Rolls Royce that you just passed in the alley.

4. Everyone who loves hamburgers and French fries. Which is why fast food joints are popping up all over town.

5. The old locomotive which was struck by the avalanche.

6. Audrey who came to her Aunt Jessica's party in her Oshkosh K-bosh overalls.

7. Mrs. Keltmeyer rescued the children from the burning house. Which was caused from a careless smoker.

8. Shawna who had been elected the president of the student council. She won a scholarship to Northern Illinois University.

9. Orestes pleaded guilty to the crime. Which shocked his parents.

10. I lent my cousin Pancho my 1973 Mustang convertible. Which was out of gas.

Punctuation Rule: To combine sentences using relative pronouns (WH words), determine if the WH clause is necessary to the meaning of the sentence. If it is necessary, no commas are needed. If the clause provides extra information not necessary to the meaning of the sentence, place commas **before** and **after** it.

Example: The house **which we bought last year** would have cost more to buy this year.
(No commas because the information is necessary. This clause is called a **restrictive** clause.)

Our neighbors, **who live in the gray house**, just adopted identical twin boys.
(Commas because the information is extra. This clause is called **non-restrictive.**)

EXERCISE 4: Combine the following sentences by using relative pronouns (WH words). First determine which group of words has the greater impact and then place a WH word before the lesser idea. After writing each sentence once, rearrange the sentence making the lesser idea in the first sentence the greater in the second. Try several in class.

Example: The dog annoyed the neighbors. He barked all night.

Combinations: The dog **which barked all night** annoyed the neighbors.
The dog **which annoyed the neighbors** barked all night.

1. My little niece kissed me gently on the cheek.
She wears braces.

74

2. Phil left for California.
   He will study Spanish architecture.

3. The *USS Springaleak* was recently launched at Burnham Harbor.
   It slid down the ramp and sank.

4. Belchmore Manor was a great place to eat.
   The chef had been trained by Count Veiner of Hamburg.

5. Mary Aileen is very dramatic.
   She produced neighborhood plays on the back porch.

6. Liz Terine was frequently shunned.
   She had "knock-em-dead" bad breath.

7. Rusty Spooks is a well known motorcycle racer.
   He donated his wheels to the local children's home.

8. Dr. I. M. Aheal revolutionized the medical world with his open toe surgery.
   He was once a famous jockey from Brazil.

9. Uncle Bill loves to fish.
   He once spent ten years as a commercial fisherman in Fontana, Wisconsin.

10. Laurel loves attending college.
    Her dad spent megabucks to send her.

SUMMARY

In **Units 2, 3, 7** and **9** you **combined** sentences with glue words, WH words, and ING words to write varied and interesting sentences and also to emphasize key ideas by subordinating lesser ideas.

As you were combining, you were also **rearranging** ideas to write varied sentence beginnings to avoid repeating the same dull sentence beginning--*The, And then, And so, I*, etc.

These writer's vocabulary skills will help you revise a first draft with the aid of the **Sentence Opening Sheet.** Also, remember that you can use the skills of **combining** and **rearranging** to correct sentence fragments.

People are natural storytellers. They enjoy narrating events in which they have participated or which they have observed.

In this paper you will tell a story as you did in the **Problem-Solving** paper. However, this time instead of telling it as a first person story, even though you might be the main character, you will tell it as if you **were an observer**.

STAGE ONE: PREWRITING

STUDENT LEARNING OBJECTIVES

1. The student will write an observation paper, using third person personal pronouns.
2. The student will limit the place, time, action, and characters of the observation.
3. The student will provide specific details, including feelings of the character(s).
4. The student will use pronouns to link ideas.

WRITING PROMPT

In an **Observing** paper you are to write a simple observation about some incident that you have experienced or observed. It does not have to be some earthshaking happening, just something that you remember vividly. The more specific details you can provide the more interesting your paper will be for your audience.

Your paper must be written in the third person point of view just as Arnie Esquivel did in the model which follows. Even if you select a personal experience, you must use the pronouns *he*, *she*, or *they* without referring to yourself directly.

Since you will be writing about a personal experience, you will be able to supply the innermost feelings of the character. The observation must be limited in time, space, character, and action so that it can be fully developed.

Now read Arnie's observation.

The Telephone Call

1. Arnie pulled the crumbled sheet of paper out of his pocket and read it, "Diane Ross 555-1025." **2.** His palms were sweating and his heart beat as if it were trying to escape his chest as he reached over to pick up the receiver. **3.** He could not open his clenched fist even though his brain said, "Do it."

4. The message would not travel to his hand. **5.** Finally, he managed to open his fist and with a shaky finger, he slowly dialed the number. **6.** Perspiration dripped from his forehead. **7.** His arms felt like lead weights. **8.** No--Arnie couldn't go through with it. **9.** He slammed the receiver to its place on the telephone.

10. Now his brain pounded back and forth screaming, "Call her, call her," over and over again.

11. His conscience kept repeating, "Call her. What do you have to lose?"

12. He really didn't have anything to lose. **13.** He had to call her and ask her to the dance before anyone else did. **14.** Once again he picked up the receiver with a shaky hand. **15.** He dialed the numbers, hoping she wasn't at home but then again praying she was. **16.** One ring, two rings, three rings passed. **17.** His heart beat furiously, and his stomach felt as if an entire butterfly population was dominating it.

18. "Hello?" her alluring voice inquired.

19. Arnie stopped breathing.

20. "Hello?" she said again.

21. Arnie wanted to say something, but his tongue stuck to the roof of his mouth.

22. "Hello, who's there?"

23. His lungs heaved to exert some kind of sound, but he stood there frozen. **24.** His head pounded and his spine tingled as his eyes swelled up with tears.

25. "Is this some kind of a joke?" her irritated voice rang through his brain.

26. He suddenly slammed the receiver down. **27.** His mind stopped and he stayed there, motionless, as if in a trance. **28.** After a minute he walked away, hating himself. **29.** He felt a little relieved, but it was going to be a long weekend!

EXERCISE 1: With your class answer the following questions:

1. How is the observation limited in time, space, character, and action?
2. Did Arnie begin with a controlling idea or did he just plunge into the action ?
3. Are the events written in a time sequence? Are there any gaps?
4. How did he glue together ideas? with transition words? pronouns?
5. What type of ending did the writer use?

SUGGESTED PERSONAL TOPICS

One of the best ways to select a topic for your observation is to hold a discussion with the class or two or three fellow students, remembering some of your strongest observations. Choose times when you felt a particularly strong emotion. Perhaps the following questions will help you get started.

1. Have you ever had a funny, or exciting, or frightening experience with a pet?
2. When was the last time you got into trouble with your parents? What happened?
3. What was the last time you were really excited about your favorite team or sport?
4. What is your favorite scene from a movie or TV show? Did it make you cringe? laugh? cry?
5. Have you ever been caught doing something really embarrassing?
6. What was the most fun you have ever had?
7. Have you ever taken a spectacular spill from your bike? a toboggan?
8. When was the last time you tried to get out of doing something you didn't want to?

WRITING ACROSS THE CURRICULUM TOPICS

1. Do you remember the first speech you had to give in front of class? How about your first audition for a play?
2. Have you ever been embarrassed by a teacher? Being caught with the wrong book? Called on when you weren't paying attention?
3. What must it have been like for the people involved in a great historical event? Lincoln at the Ford Theater? Hannibal as he crossed the mountains? Eve as she offered Adam a bite of her apple? Some historical topics may demand some research on your part because you need to be familiar with the details of the event. You do have, however, poetic license to imagine the feelings of the people involved.

4. What were your feelings in biology when you had to dissect a frog? What were the steps you used in chemistry to create the worst smell in the world?
5. Did you ever sew something in Home Economics that turned out really awful? Did you ever sand your project so well there was no wood left?
6. What are your most vivid memories of Driver's Education? What vital lessons did you learn?

THINK SHEET

After you have selected your topic, you need to explore it to see if you have enough information and/or details to write this paper. In a concrete way this **Think Sheet** will help you to review the events of your observation.

Remember that your audience does **not** know anything about your observation. Your job is to make the story interesting by recounting the events and sharing the feelings. Colorful adjectives, adverbs, and verbs will aid you in creating a realistic incident in which your audience can share.

Even before you begin filling out the **Think Sheet**, you might want to draw a picture of the scene. This might help you recall specific details. You might also describe this observation to a classmate or in a cooperative learning group. These are additional prewriting strategies.

Name_____

Observing Think Sheet

1. What type of observation are you going to *narrate*?

   _____

2. Specific time covered_____

3. Specific place_____

4. Specific action_____

5. Specific participants_____

6. Jot down all the actions that took place in the beginning, the middle, and the end of your incident. With each action mark down the specific details that occurred. Expand with journalistic questions. Talk over your ideas with a friend.

| **Specific Actions** | **Specific Details** |

A. Beginning

   1._____

   2._____

   3._____

B. Middle

   1._____

   2._____

   3._____

C. Ending

   1._____

   2._____

   3._____

CONTROLLING IDEA

You have three choices to begin this composition. First, you may write a general statement of what will be proven by your observation. Second, you can jump right into the action of the incident and save your controlling idea as the clincher sentence of your paper. Third, you may have an inferred controlling idea, that is, an unstated controlling idea where the total content of the paper conveys the message. **The Telephone Call** on page 77 is a good example of the third option.

Example Introductory Paragraph

If you are writing a multi-paragraph paper, a background information paragraph will make a good introduction. Here is a sample:

Learning the Hard Way

A student will undergo many frustrating moments in her high school career. Sometimes she will learn from these events and be the better person because of them. On other occasions she is not able to cope with them or bounce back from them. Patty Jo MacKenzie learned that **losers can gain more than winners** when she hit the serve into the net in the conference championship game against Wyoming High School.

Notice that in this sample introductory paragraph the writer includes her controlling idea as well as information, which leads up to the event she is going to describe.

ORGANIZING THE PAPER

Organize your ideas in the actual time sequence in which they occurred. In writing your first draft, you will probably add bits of information that you will recall as the ideas begin to flow.

If you are writing a multi-paragraph paper, each time sequence can be a paragraph. If you are writing a single paragraph, you will organize in a before, during, and ending sequence in one paragraph.

POINT OF VIEW

Although you will most likely be writing about a personal experience, you should write this paper in the third person point of view. Write as though you are observing yourself. Third person personal pronouns should be used. Refer to yourself by name (or make up a fictitious name--here is your chance to try out that name you always wished you had!) or by third person pronouns.

THIRD PERSON PERSONAL PRONOUNS:
Singular: he, she, it, him, her, his, her, its
Plural: they, them, their, theirs

GLUING TOGETHER IDEAS

Since this paper will be following a definite time sequence, make sure that you use transition words that show time. You may also link ideas by repeating pronouns or key words that refer back to persons or objects already mentioned just as Arnie did by referring to himself as "he."

TRANSITION WORDS:
once, then, when, first, today, soon, while, yesterday, before, after, early, later, since, finally, suddenly, gradually, thus, further, etc.

EXERCISE 1: Read the following student model, then substitute pronouns for the name Julie Jablonski. This will help you see how pronouns can be used to glue together ideas.

Caught

Julie Jablonski leisurely leaned back against the ugly, pink bathroom stall wall and took a deep drag of Julie Jablonski's cigarette. For the first time in the entire chaotic school day, Julie Jablonski could relax.

White smoke lazily lapped above Julie Jablonski's head and gradually drifted around the twelve-stall bathroom. This peaceful daydreaming state of mind was shattered almost immediately. Julie Jablonski heard the clicking of high-heeled shoes, which could only signify a teacher walking outside the bathroom.

Quickly Julie Jablonski shut the stall door, threw Julie Jablonski's cigarette into the toilet, and violently swished Julie Jablonski's hands back and forth to relieve the air of any remaining smoke. Unfortunately, the clicking of high shoes sounded as if they walked into the bathroom. Julie Jablonski's stomach dropped and a lump in Julie Jablonski's throat would not go away. Julie Jablonski realized the bathroom had been filled with smoke before Julie Jablonski closed the stall door.

All of a sudden Julie Jablonski froze, for the clicking stopped. Slowly, against Julie Jablonski's will, Julie Jablonski lowered her eyes only to see a pair of stern black shoes that had thick legs attached to them right underneath Julie Jablonski's stall door. Standing there half frozen, Julie Jablonski could not take her eyes away from those black shoes.

"Oh! *$%@*!" Julie Jablonski thought to herself.

"This is Sister Eucalyptus speaking, and whoever is in there had better come out right this second!"

"No." Julie Jablonski muttered.

"What do you mean 'No' ? Is this Julie Jablonski?"

"Sister, I've had a tough day, so just leave me alone. Please."

Sister Eucalyptus' face relaxed as she unsuccessfully tried to convince Julie to come out.

"Okay, Julie," she finally said. "I'll let you go this time, but don't let me catch you again or you'll get the five detentions you deserve."

Sister Eucalyptus left the bathroom more amused than defeated. Julie Jablonski sighed with relief as Julie Jablonski lighted another cigarette.

Note: Caught was written by a student about a real incident in her life. She captured the specific, true feelings involved in this personal experience. However, the next time Julie Jablonski (not her real name) attempted to "relax" in the bathroom, she was not so fortunate--two Saturday "Breakfast Club" meetings.

ENDING

You should plan an ending to this paper just as you plan your opening. Your final event may leave a lasting impression so that you need not supply any other comment. Also, you may write a short statement summarizing the meaning of the incident.

If your introduction begins with a controlling idea, your last sentence could then serve as the clincher. Here is an example:

> . . . The ball spun and plunged itself into the core of the basket.
> It hesitated momentarily, bounced against the back of the rim, and circled
> the rim like a roulette ball. The basket erupted and vomited the ball out.
> **Charles experienced the most frustrating moment of his life.**

If you are writing a multi-paragraph paper, you may wish to write a concluding paragraph which either makes a comment or summarizes. Whatever you decide, make sure that the ending leaves the reader with the feeling that your observation is over. Make sure, too, that the reader is left with the one dominant impression you want him to feel.

STAGE TWO: WRITING THE FIRST DRAFT

With your **Think Sheet** in front of you, write your first draft. Skip every other line and number your sentences. Do not worry about mechanical errors at this point. Just put your words onto paper. You can make corrections later.

Here are some short-term goals to keep in mind:

1. Begin with a general statement about what will be proven, or plunge directly into the action or by inferring a controlling idea.
2. Organize the observation into a beginning, middle, and end sequence.
3. Include specific details so that the audience shares in your experience or observation. Be an author--get into the feelings of the character(s).
4. Use past tense, concrete verbs. Verb Power!
5. Use transition words or pronouns to glue together ideas.
6. End with a satisfying finality.
7. If you use dialogue, study the punctuation rules on pages 181-182.

Now write the first draft.

STAGE THREE: REWRITING

SENTENCE OPENING SHEET

After you have finished your first draft, fill out the **Sentence Opening Sheet** according to your teacher's instructions. Be sure to note what combining, rearranging, subtracting, expanding and correcting you want to make when you revise.

Pages 13-15 provide a complete explanation of the **SOS** sheet.

Since this composition is being written in third person point of view, you might want to use the special column to list personal pronouns. This will help you discover if you shifted your reference from third person (*he, she, it*) to second person (*you*) to first person (*I*).

PEER EVALUATION USING A CHECKLIST SHEET

As you evaluate your partner's paper, remember to treat her paper as though it were your own. You would appreciate as much help as possible and so will your partner.

Also, if your partner's paper includes dialogue and you are not sure of the punctuation rules, pages 181-182 provide some examples.

Writer's Name_____

Corrector's Name_____

Observing Checklist Sheet

1. What type of beginning did the writer use--plunging into the action of the observation or writing a formal controlling idea?

2. Are the events organized in a logical sequence?

3. Does each event lead to the next? In other words, are there any gaps? Does the reader need to know more about a particular situation?

4. Circle all the pronouns the writer used to link ideas together. Make sure the reference for each pronoun is clear.

5. What type of ending did the writer use?

6. Do any sentences need to be combined and/or rearranged for variety in the sentence openings and structures?

7. If dialogue was used, check to see that the writer punctuated correctly.

8. Which one suggestion would you make to improve this composition?

STAGE FOUR: PUBLISHING

Make your final draft error-free. Before submitting it to your teacher, read it aloud one more time. See if it meets the objectives listed on page 76.

Share your observation with a classmate or with students in another class who are writing observation papers.

If your school publishes a literary magazine, you may want to submit your composition for publication.

You might want to include this piece of writing in your portfolio.

Business letters are important means of communication. In your future you will probably write many types of business letters: letters of application for a job, letters of complaint about damaged merchandise, or letters of request for information about college admissions or playoff tickets for your local sports team.

PARTS OF A BUSINESS LETTER

Heading

There are six parts to business letters: heading, inside address, greeting, body, complimentary close, and the signature. The heading is the writer's complete mailing or return address. It is placed at least one and one-half inches from the top of the paper. The date is immediately below the address. The month should be spelled out, not abbreviated.

Examples:

9682 Heinritz Road	7705 Dalewood Parkway
Poygan, WI 54843	Bolingbrook, IL 60515
May 20, 2005	October 4, 2001

Inside Address

The inside address includes the name of the person you are writing to and his complete mailing address. A person's name in the inside address should be prefaced with a courtesy title such as Mr., Mrs., or Ms. If you are writing to a company and the person has an official title, put the title after the name or below the name.

Example: Mrs. Agnes Budz or Mrs. Agnes Budz, President
President
Wenbin Cleaning Services
16318 S. Ridgeland Avenue
Tinley Park, Illinois 60477

Here is an example of an inside address when the name is not known.

Cahreb Industries
123 New Brunswick Avenue
Palatine, Texas 74321

Salutation or Greeting

The salutation is a greeting. It is always followed by a colon. When the name of the person is known, you should use these greetings: **Dear Mr. Baldelli:**; **Dear Ms. Kavanaugh:**.

When writing to an individual whose name is not known, use **Dear Sir:**. When writing a department head or company, use **Gentlemen:**.

Body

The body is the most important part of the letter. Here you state your message in a clear and direct manner.

Your paragraphs should be short so that your reader can easily spot the main points. Unnecessary details will only clutter up your message. Avoid clichés and trite expressions such as *on this memorable occasion, it gives me a great deal of pleasure* or *far be it for me to say.* **YUK**!

The tone of your letter should be pleasant and courteous. A *please* and a *thank you* go a long way.

Complimentary Close

The complimentary close indicates the closing of the letter. Typical closings are "**S**incerely yours**,**" "**Y**ours truly**,**" and "**C**ordially yours." The first word is always capitalized. The last word is followed by a comma.

Signature

The last basic part of the letter is the signature. The choice of including your middle name or initial is yours. You should use the signature that you would write in all your business transactions.

If your letter is typewritten, your name should be written in longhand between the complimentary close and the typewritten signature. If the letter is not typed, handwrite your name, then print your name underneath just in case your handwriting is not legible.

A courtesy title should be used before a woman's name. At times an identification title may be used that indicates the position in the company of the individual signing the letter.

Handwritten Signature

Sincerely yours

Scott J. Zigmond

Scott J. Zigmond

Courtesy Title

Yours truly

Dianne Heinritz

(Mrs. Diane Heinritz)

Identification Title

Cordially yours,

Iris Stone

Iris Stone

Vice President

Envelopes

The outside address found on the envelope should be identical to the inside address found in the letter. Write or type the name and address of the addressee on the lower half of the envelope. Your name and address should appear in the upper left-hand corner. Put the stamp in the upper right-hand corner.

Billy Jo Youngman
1020 Belmont Avenue
Harmony, OH 45502

stamp

Mr. Leo Ringgold
Saturn Fireworks, Inc.
100 Wilshire Lane
Elsanor, AL 36567

STUDENT MODEL

Before selecting the type of business letter you will be writing, read the following student model letter of complaint:

Heading	↔	12646 S. 69th Ct. Palos Heights, IL 60453 December 12, 2005

Customer Service Department Dexter Shoe Corporation 114 Railroad Avenue Dexter, ME 04930	↔	**Inside Address**

To Whom It May Concern:	↔	**Greeting or Salutation**

My entire family, especially my dad, enjoys wearing your shoes. They are always comfortable and look great, too. I recently bought a pair of your shoes, and I think they're great; they feel good and are rather cute. I just love to wear them everywhere.

B
O However, shortly after I bought them, I noticed some wear and tear that should
D not occur. I had only worn them twice, so naturally, I felt very disappointed
Y when I noticed this. The thread on the tip of my left shoe began to tear, causing the sole to come apart from the rest of the shoe.

I was wondering if there is anything your company can do because I would like to have this pair to wear. I hope you will contact me about what to do. If you would like me to send them back, I will because they were expensive.

As I mentioned before, I hope something can be done about this because I do like the shoes, and I have never experienced a problem like this before.

Sincerely,	↔	**Complimentary Close**

Juli Barcelona

Juli Barcelona	↔	**Signature**

STAGE ONE: PREWRITING

STUDENT LEARNING OBJECTIVES

1. The student will write a business letter.
2. The student will include six parts in the business letter: the heading, the inside address, the greeting, the body, the closing, and the signature.
3. The student will punctuate correctly.
4. The student will capitalize the correct words.
5. The student will prepare an envelope correctly for the letter.

WRITING PROMPTS

Since real life situations often require you to write a business letter, you will be given many options for this assignment. As a class activity, review the situations from the various topics.

1. Write a letter of complaint about some discourteous service or poor treatment you have experienced as a customer.

2. Write a letter of application to an employer in your area and request a job interview. Ideas to include in the letter: job you are applying for; where you heard about the job; your personal qualifications including work experience; personal references; request for interview.

3 . Write a letter of complaint concerning some damaged merchandise you received. Ideas to include: problem with merchandise; action called for on the part of the company.

4. Write a letter of request to a college asking for a college catalog and an application.

5. Write a letter to the editor of your local newspaper, responding to a local controversial issue.

6. Write a letter requesting information from a well-known individual.

7. Write a letter to one of your teachers, trying to persuade her to give you a good grade for your work. Since you want good grades for all of your classes, any teacher will do as the audience for your letter.

ORGANIZING THE LETTER

In a business letter you should begin by immediately letting your reader know the purpose of your letter in a straightforward and direct manner.

The organization of your letter will depend upon its purpose. For example, if you are writing a letter of request about college information, you should first identify yourself and explain your specific interest. Then you should request the specific information you are requesting, e. g., catalogs which provide information on courses, tuition, fees, etc.

If you are writing a letter of complaint, you should state your problem clearly in the first paragraph of the body of the letter. The remaining paragraphs should explain the attempts you tried to solve this problem and the specific action you would like to company to take to resolve this dilemma.

You must make sure you include all the necessary facts and details, and write in an honest and natural style.

Your tone should be courteous and positive throughout the letter.

Your paragraphs should be short and to the point.

THINK SHEET

There is no *standard* **Think Sheet** for this letter. The type of business letter you are writing controls the organization. You need to create your own. However, you should still brainstorm ideas on a scratch paper.

Here are some ideas to consider:

- Purpose of your letter
- Complete address of person to whom you are writing
- Information you are requesting
- Problem you encountered/attempts made/action requested
- One main thought per paragraph
- Tone

STAGE TWO: WRITING THE FIRST DRAFT

Before you begin to write your letter, review the proper form for a business letter.

Now write your letter.

STAGE THREE: REWRITING

Before you rewrite your final draft, exchange your letter with a partner or share it in your cooperative learning group.

Try this oral reading procedure:

- One member of the team should read the letter aloud to the other team members.

- The team members should discuss the following points:
    a. What is the purpose of the letter?
    b. Is the letter easy to follow?
    c. Does the writer need to include more supportive ideas? Why or why not?
    d. What is the tone of the letter?
    e. What did you like best about the letter?

PEER EVALUATION USING A CHECKLIST SHEET

In addition to the oral checking, have your partner answer the questions on the **Checklist Sheet.**

Writer's Name_____

Corrector's Name_____

Business Letter Checklist Sheet

1. What is the writer's purpose in the letter?

2. Did the writer follow the business letter format? If not, mark the spots on the first draft.

3. Is each paragraph in the body of the fully developed? If not, mark the weak spots on the first draft.

4. Did the writer include any unnecessary details that could be subtracted? If so, put the symbol **YUK** or **REP** above them on the first draft.

5. What type of tone did the writer maintain throughout the letter?

6. What one suggestion you would make for the writer to improve the letter?

STAGE FOUR: PUBLISHING

Since business letters are written to a specific audience, your publishing activity for this unit is to send the letter. Don't forget the stamp.

You might also want to include this letter in your writing portfolio.

Just as the ING word conveys the notion of motion, the ED word describes a stationary or permanent situation. A **broken** windowpane, a **ruptured** football, and a **varnished** desk remain that way forever. In writing the **Describing Spatially** paper in the next unit, you will describe a room by using ED words as adjectives to describe the objects that are in a stationary or permanent situation.

You have already learned how to use ED words to indicate past tense in writing the **Problem-Solving** paper and the **Observing** paper. Now you will learn how to use them as adjectives. Note, however, that not all past participles end in ED, e. g., brok**en**, los**t**, stol**en**.

Past participles that end in ED are regular verbs. Past participles that end in *t, nt, en,* or *ht,* etc. are irregular verbs. You probably memorized a list of these regular and irregular verbs in junior high school when you studied principal parts of verbs.

Examples:

- The mailman **delivered** the package. (Past tense)
- The **delivered** package contains history books. (Adjective--past participle)
- The package **delivered** by the mailman contains history books.
     (Adjective--past participle)

- The leaves **were strewn** about by the wind. (Verb)
- The **wind-strewn** leaves swirled around the yard. (Adjective)
- The criminal **caught** by the little old lady received a three-year sentence.
     (Adjective--past participle)

Whether you realize it or not, you constantly use ED words to describe objects and persons in your daily conversations.

Examples:

fried potatoes	**buttered** popcorn	**tossed** salad
rugged individual	**vacuumed** carpet	**damaged** property
pool **filled** with water	windows **closed** by the wind	car **washed** by hand
sun burnt face	**embarrassed** sophomores	desk **cluttered** with papers
fired manager	diamond **cut** to order	**forgotten** song
peppers **filled** with rice	wind-**blown** confetti	smoke-**filled** room

Can you think of ED words used to describe objects and people that are part of your everyday vocabulary? As a group activity, make a list of ED words that describe objects and people. How about a **fallen** angel, an **exhausted** worker, **salted** popcorn **smothered** with hot butter? Make a list of fifty ED word clusters.

EXERCISE 1: **Expand** the following ED words by adding details from a room in your house whenever possible. The examples are in **bold**.

1. toppled

2. stained **(mud-stained jeans)**

3. strewn

4. stacked

5. carpeted

6. dusted

7. swept **(recently swept floor)**

8. varnished

9. packed

10. oval-shaped

11. cluttered

12. assorted **(assorted memorabilia lay sandwiched between the desk and the glass top)**

13. old-fashioned

14. smudged

15. piled

16. painted

17. stapled **(stapled student handbook)**

18. polished

19. shelved

20. perched

21. littered

22. shoes

23. multi-colored

24. torn

25. mattressed **(mattressed between two books)**

SENSE APPEALING WORD CLUSTERS

Just as you used ING words to describe a storm in the **Describing Chronologically** unit, you should try to include ED word clusters in the next paper.

EXERCISE 2: Subtract unnecessary empty words by rearranging sentence parts and expanding when necessary. Try to write sentences using ED word clusters to describe a particular object. Be careful of fragments caused by ED words and WH words. Each completed sentence should contain a present tense verb.

Example: The bed **which is** being covered by a quilt **which is** made of the skin **which is** that of a leopard.

Sample Word Clusters: The leopard-skin, quilt-covered bed *(expand)* sits in the northeast corner next to the radiator.

A leopard skin (***present tense verb*) covers** the bed.

1. **There is** a wall **which is** north and **which is** dark and **which is** oak and **which is** paneled **which has** a moose **which is** hanging and **which is** stuffed and **which is** in the middle of it.

2. **There is** a bed **which is** soft and **which is** white and **which has** a mattress **which is** on top of it.

3. The bed **which is** being covered by a blanket **which is** made of cotton.

4. **There** sits a dresser **which is** old and **which is** small and **which is** varnished **which has** stickers **which are** of forest preserves and **which are** of different vacation spots.

5. **There is** a closet **which is** holding a jacket **which i**s for hunting and the closet has a large door **which** folds.

6. **There is** a television **which is** colored and **which is** a Zenith **which is** standing just a few feet to the left of the bookcase and the television **which is** facing a head of a moose **which is** staring.

7. **There is** a wall **which is** paneled **which is** made of grain **which is** dark and **which is** oak.

8. **There is** a case **which** holds books **which** has doors **which** are made of glass **which is** old.

DANGLING AND MISPLACED MODIFIERS

In the **Describing Spatially** unit which follows, you will describe a room totally devoid of people. In other words, you must write from the camera's viewpoint. Therefore, you will have to be careful in using present participles (ING words) because they could result in dangling and misplaced modifiers.

You should also avoid using the command form of the verb. When the command form of the verb is used, it implies that a person must perform the action. Since no people are allowed in this composition, the command form of the verb cannot be used.

Here are three uses of ING words:

Position Words:	hanging, sitting, standing, resting, containing, etc.
Descriptive Words:	glistening windows, sliding doors, blowing curtains, etc.
Action Words:	walking through the door, entering the room, looking around the corner, etc.

The first two uses are possible in this paper. The last one could result in dangling and misplaced modifiers.

EXERCISE 3: When you write ING action words in your spatial description, be careful that they are not dangling or misplaced. If they are misplaced, you must rearrange and expand to correct the error. In the following sentences identify the error and then rewrite the corrected sentences on a separate sheet of paper.

Example: Screaming loudly, the truck knocked the frightened lady to the ground.

Who is screaming loudly? The truck?

Revised: Screaming loudly, the frightened lady was knocked to the ground by a truck.

Example: Looking into the room, an orange and yellow refrigerator sits in the northeast corner.

Who is looking into the room? The refrigerator?

Revised: An orange and yellow refrigerator sits in the northeast corner of the room.

1. Looking out the window, the squirrel gathered up nuts for the winter.

2. Walking with a stick in his hand, the collie was led by his master.

3. Rounding the corner abruptly, my hat blew off in the wind.

4. While teeing off at the 18th hole, a snake slithered across the fairway.

5. Galloping through Central Park, the police captured the runaway pony.

6. Running with high knee action, the camera caught the scampering halfback.

7. With its flaps down, the signal officer guided the attack bomber to the deck of the carrier.

8. Ditching class regularly, the truant officer nabbed the delinquent student in Pinkey's Snack Shop.

9. Exhausted from the long walk, the worn out shoes had a huge hole in their sole.

10. Leaking profusely, the plumber fixed the leak in the sink.

11. Having been killed in the accident, the ambulance brought the dead body to the morgue.

12. Yelling for help, the tree struck by lightning pinned the helpless girl.

13. After walking from the room with downcast eyes, the corpse was prepared for the funeral by the undertaker.

14. After three years of captivity, Tiny Tommy was rescued from his attic cell by the police wearing tattered rags.

15. To write effectively, a teacher requires two drafts of every student's composition.

SUMMARY

ED words can be used as verbs to show action or as adjectives to describe a person or object. If ING words and ED words are used as modifiers, they must be located as close as possible to the words they modify. Otherwise, the sentence's meaning can become confusing. Actually, some of these misplaced and dangling modifiers can cause some "funny" sentences.

One of the keys to being a good writer is to convey to your audience in words what you see with your eyes. You'll practice that strategy in this writing assignment.

STAGE ONE: PREWRITING

STUDENT LEARNING OBJECTIVES

1. The student will write a controlling idea that identifies the room being described.
2. The student will organize the ideas spatially, moving from right to left, left to right, foreground to background, etc
3. The student will describe the items with specific details using past participles (ED words) whenever possible.
4. The student will link ideas using spatial transition words.
5. The student will end by commenting on the room's appearance.

WRITING PROMPTS

The topic of this paper is your bedroom. Your composition must be written from a strictly camera viewpoint which eliminates any first person reference.

You have several options in describing your room. First, you could describe the bedroom after you and your friends have *destroyed* its appearance. In this situation the bedroom's description would center on the room being in a state of disorder and chaos.

Second, you could describe the room just after it has been immaculately cleaned for your Aunt Babuska's stay at hour home. Everything is in its place with not a speck of dust anywhere.

Third, you could describe your room so that it reveals a dominant trait of your personality. Would a visitor immediately notice how neat you are? How messy you are? That you like a particular color? That you are afraid of the dark? That you like to study or read?

Finally, you could describe your room showing your multi-interests. If somebody walked into your room and looked around, what could they immediately tell about your interests? Would they see posters of Chicago Bulls' players? Would they see a collection of baseball pennants? Would they see pictures of relatives and friends? Would they see stacks of tapes and CD's?

Whatever choice you make, you must stick to that particular topic so that you give a single indelible impression. Keep in mind that first impressions are important. You will have plenty to do if you include all the minute details which support your main idea. After all, your purpose is to create a vivid impression of your bedroom. The same thing is true if you decide to choose another topic.

Of course, many other topics lend themselves to the spatial development organizational pattern, but to choose another topic, you first need to get your teacher's approval.

OTHER TOPICS

1. Furnish a room: Suppose that a long lost rich uncle, Lord Thorgood Clively, III, left you $25,000 with the stipulation that the money could only be used to design the room of your choice. Design the room.

2. Computer room: The local school district has asked you to design a computer office for Ms. Rom Disk.

3. Drama: a. Design a stage for the drama department of the new school being built in your neighborhood.
          b. Describe a one-room setting for a play such as *The Death of a Salesman* or for some other specific play perhaps from William Shakespeare.

4. Picture: Choose a picture of a room you like in a decorating magazine (e. g., *Better Homes and Garden*) and write a description of it. Your Home Economics teacher might suggest this topic.

5. Personal dream: A green house, a garage workshop, a basement rec room, a room at a special time of year, the ideal school classroom. (Your teacher would like that!)

6. Science: Describe a place you visited on a recent field trip such as a planetarium, a museum, a laboratory, etc.

7.   Art: Describe an art gallery, a pottery factory, a ceramics shop, etc.

8. History: Describe a battlefield just after the battle has ended.
    (e. g. After Custer's defeat!)

9. Driver's Education: Describe the scene of an accident you have either
    been in or have seen.

10.   Miscellaneous: a. Design a playground or playhouse for your little
                            brother or sister.
                        b. Describe the school cafeteria at the end of lunch
                            before the custodian has started cleanup.
                        c. Describe the school corridor on the last day of
                            school when the students have just gone after
                            emptying their lockers.
                        d. Think of your favorite TV or movie star,
                            or sports celebrity. You have been contracted by
                            that individual to design a special room in their
                            new $10,000,000 home. Go ahead and design that
                            unique room.

THINK SHEET

So far you have practiced different prewriting strategies in the
prewriting stage: 1) talking to a friend about your topic; 2) drawing a picture
of an observation; and 3) answering questions on a **Think Sheet**.

For this assignment, a sketch, drawing, or picture of the room you
decide to describe should serve as your brainstorming guide.

To recall the exact location of each item in the room, complete this
Think Sheet as you are sitting there or at least have a picture in front of you.
Or if you are designing an imaginary room, let your creative juices flow.
Have fun.

On a separate sheet of paper, describe each item, using, if possible,
some of the ED word clusters you wrote for the first few exercises from **Unit 12**.

Name_____

Describing Spatially Think Sheet

1. Draw a rough sketch of the room placing items in their proper place.

2. What is the object that you are using as your focal point?

3. In what part of the room is this object located?

4. What type of room are you going to describe?

5. Tentative controlling idea

CONTROLLING IDEA

In the **Problem-Solving** paper you wrote a stated controlling idea. It was probably the first sentence of your paper or was located in the introduction. In the **Describing Chronologically** paper you used an inferred or nonstated controlling idea by immediately setting the scene.

For this composition you should write a stated controlling idea. It probably will be the first sentence of your paper if you are writing a single paragraph and will leave your reader with an impression of the type of person who inhabits the room.

Controlling Idea: In the center of the north wall hangs a high intensity lamp which peers down on the many pens, pencils, theme papers, reference books, and recent issues of *Time* magazine cluttered about the scholar's sturdy, mahogany desk.

In this controlling idea the writer used the high intensity lamp peering down on a desk as the focal point. It also gives the impression of the room's inhabitant as being a scholar.

If you are writing a multi-paragraph, the controlling idea will be a part of the introductory paragraph. A background information introduction might be appropriate for this paper.

Example:

Aunt Mellie lives in Anchorage, Alaska, so it isn't often that she comes to visit. Whenever she does decide to make the long journey, it is absolutely imperative that the house be spotless from attic to basement. That means that the O'Neally family spends several days toiling away removing the litter and grime which have collected during the normal day to day routine. **My room, which often resembles Theo Huxtable's from *The Bill Cosby Show*, now looks like it would be a teenager's model room for a pictorial feature   in *House and Garden*.**

ORGANIZING THE PAPER

The room's description must be organized from left to right, right to left, foreground to background, etc. The audience must be able to place each item in its proper place.

If you are writing a multi-paragraph paper, an easy way to organize the paper into paragraphs is to make the description of each wall into a separate paragraph. If you are using one of the alternative topics, you can divide paragraphs by the sections of space or the items you are describing. For instance, you could describe each room of the museum or art gallery you visited; or you could describe the various items left in the wake of Custer's battle.

Here is a brief list of items that might be included in your description:

furniture, wood paneling, windows, building materials, curtains, magazine racks, shoe racks, CD player, televisions, souvenirs, tables, model airplanes, dolls, paintings, sports equipment, family pictures, statues, trophies, posters, memorabilia, combs, brushes, colognes, collector's items, dressers, beds, rugs, closets, cabinets, computer table, etc.

VERB POWER

So that you do not confuse past tense verbs and past participles, write this paper in the present tense. For some verbs, the past tense form and the past participle form are the same. Review page 97 in the previous unit for examples:

Here is a brief list of verbs that might help you in writing the paper:

rests, lies, lays, sits, stands, contains, covers, surrounds, hangs, situates, positions, separates, occupies, leans, encloses, overlaps, piles, cuts, ends, overhangs, stretches, clamps, shines, holds, flanks, hides, peaks, protects, extends, clings, faces, displays, emits, etc.

All the forms of the verb are third person singular. To form the third person plural, simply subtract the *s*.

Example:

Singular: A book **rests** on the table.
Plural: Two books **rest** on the table. A book and a pen **rest** on the table.

GLUING TOGETHER IDEAS

In this paper you must use transition words to point out where different objects in the room are located. Here is a list of transition words that indicate place:

> **TRANSITION WORDS (Spatial):**
> underneath, above, between, below, farther, across, here, there, beyond, nearby, opposite to, on top of, left, right, behind, next to, upon, directly opposite, north, south, northeast corner, etc.

ENDING

Your paper must not just stop but must flow naturally out of the room's description. In this paper you might sum up the description by rephrasing the controlling and dominant impression of the room. You may also return to your focal point where you began your description.

STUDENT MODEL

Before writing your first draft, study the student model. Answer the following questions.

1. Does the first sentence locate the focal point?
2. What is the object the writer used?
3. Does the first sentence indicate the impression the writer is trying to create? What is it?
4. Is the paper organized spatially?
5. What transition words indicate place?
6. What ED words are used to describe the objects in the room?
7. Are there any dangling modifiers because of ING words? How can you correct them?
8. Are the verbs in the present tense?
9. How did the paper end?

The Christmas Room

1. Glistening brightly in the corner of the room stands an enormous Christmas tree. **2.** Its bright, vivid, flashing lights illuminate the cheerful room, and the shiny, glittering sparkling tinsel adds to the mood. **3.** Colorful ornaments hang on the tree like cut glass in a kaleidoscope while the star on top shines like Haley's comet in the heavens.

4. Below the evergreen tree circles a family train set with last minute Christmas shoppers riding aboard the locomotive. **5. Displayed** on the table to the right sit beautifully **wrapped** packages and gifts that children eagerly await to open.
6. Positioned above the doorway to the kitchen, which is adjacent to the family room, hangs freshly cut mistletoe. **7.** Its beauty and history ask for lovers to come kiss under it.
8. The fragrant, green, seasonal plant draws people together like children flock to fresh, out-of-the-oven, warm cookies.

9. Centered perfectly on the south wall rests the navy, leather couch, now **decorated** with green and red pillows for the holiday. **10.** Warm, toasty, billowing air ruffles the curtains to the left of the sofa. **11.** These curtains and the window pane they surround keep out the chilly, blustery, cold December weather.

12. Next comes the heart of the room. **13.** This huge, gorgeous, brick-red fireplace not only proves a place for stockings to be hung but also *calls* for the family.
14. The fireplace's burning, crackling, fiery flame gives off warmth, comfort, and love.
15. The family cat snuggles warmly on a soft leather recliner chair to the right of the hearth.

16. On the floor below, **surrounded** by all these cheery, gay, festive decorations stretches the antique Christmas carpet that Grandma crocheted over forty years ago. **17.** Above the French doors on the north wall is a fancy evergreen garland with bright, flashy, colorful Christmas lights **entwined** in it. **18.** It matches the Christmas tree perfectly. **19.** This scene creates a comfortable, relaxed, cheery atmosphere that really depicts the Christmas spirit.

STAGE TWO: WRITING THE FIRST DRAFT

With your rough sketch of your room in front of you, write your first draft. Try to include as many ED words clusters as possible to describe the various objects so that your room is "camera ready" for the reader. Remember, your purpose is to make your reader "see" your room and to use ED words as adjectives.

Also, if you begin your sentences with ING words, be careful to avoid dangling and misplaced modifiers.

Here are some ideas to consider as you write your first draft:

1. Begin with a controlling idea that names an object as a focal point and locates the object for your reader.
2 Organize your ideas spatially, left to right, right to left, foreground to background, etc.
3.   Describe your room's items with specific details. When possible, use ED words.
4. Use transition words to link ideas.
5. Keep all your verbs in the present tense.
6. End by returning to the starting point or by making some commentary about the room.

Now write the first draft.

STAGE THREE: REWRITING

SENTENCE OPENING SHEET

After you complete your **Sentence Opening Sheet**, check each column for the following:

Column One   **First Four Words Per Sentence**

1. Do all of my sentences begin with directions such as "To the left of the dresser" or "To the right of the . . . "? Can I rearrange them to make my openings more interesting?
2. Do any of my sentences begin with ING words? Are those sentence openers dangling or misplaced modifiers?

Column Two   Special

1. Do I include ED words as adjectives describing various objects in the room?

    Note: To check to see if you used ED words, list your ED words in the special column. If none are listed, maybe you need to expand with some ED words on your final draft.

Column Three   Verbs

1. Are all my verbs in the present tense?
2. Did I repeat the same verbs over and over, e. g., **sits**, **stands**, etc.?
3. Do all my singular verbs have singular subjects? Plural verbs-plural subjects? Check for subject-verb agreement!

Special Hint: To check for errors in subject-verb agreement, find the verb and ask yourself *what is it that* **rests**, **sits**, **stands**, **occupies**, *etc.?* If the verb ends in *s*, there should be only one "what." If the verb does not end in an "s," there should be more than one "what."

Column Four   Number of Words Per Sentence

1. Are any of my longer sentences run-ons?
2. Is there variety in my sentence lengths?

PEER EVALUATION USING A CHECKLIST SHEET

Before you answer the questions on the **Checklist Sheet**, first read your partner's paper through two or three times to become familiar with the content. Then without looking at your partner's **Think Sheet**, draw a sketch of the room. Compare your drawing with the original **Think Sheet**.

Describing Spatially Checklist Sheet

1. What is the object the writer located in the controlling idea that serves as the focal point? What is the impression the writer is trying to create? Is the room in disorder? Is the inhabitant a music lover, a sports fanatic? Is the room immaculate? Does the room reflect the many interests of its occupant?

2. Is the paper organized spatially--right to left, left to right, foreground to background, etc.?

3. If you had a difficult time locating objects, maybe the writer did not use transition words properly. Circle the transition words on the first draft.

4. Which objects need to be expanded with more sensory descriptions to get a fuller view of the room?

5. Did the ending leave you with an impression of the type of person who lives in this room?

6. Are all the verbs in the present tense? Does the writer repeat the same weak verbs? If so, offer some suggestions.

7. Do the sentences begin with the same pattern? If a sentence begins with an ING word, is that sentence a dangling or misplaced modifier?

8. What one suggestion would you make for the writer to improve the composition?

STAGE FOUR: PUBLISHING

Along with your final draft, include a drawing or picture of your room. Put in on a poster board.

Select the best descriptions and send them to ***Better Homes and Garden*** magazine.

Some of you might want to include your description in your writing portfolio.

Just as in your overall organization of your persuasive essay in the next unit you will rank your ideas in an order of importance sequence, you will also learn to rank ideas within a sentence. This skill is called **subordination**. **Subordination** is a specific type of sentence combining in which you emphasize important ideas over less important ideas. Important ideas are complete thoughts and could be written as separate sentences.

> Baby Ellisa smiled at her mother.
> Stacey laboriously collated the envelopes.

Lesser ideas cannot stand by themselves; they depend on some other part of the sentence for meaning.

> While bathing in the tub.
> As she watched "All My Children."

Combining the important idea with the less important idea enables the writer to indicate the relationship of ideas.

> While bathing in the tub, baby Ellisa smiled at her mother.

> Stacey laboriously collated the envelopes as she watched
> "All My Children."

In the earlier units of *Stack the Deck* you practiced subordinating lesser ideas. Now we want you to concentrate on using all the different sentence structures you have been taught to emphasize main ideas. In this way when you want to stress a specific idea as you revise a first draft, you can subordinate properly.

SUBORDINATING LESSER IDEAS

EXERCISE 1: On a separate sheet of paper, rewrite the following sentences, introducing the lesser ideas with subordinating conjunctions (glue words), relative pronouns (WH words), present participles (ING words), and/or past participles (ED words). The important idea in each sentence should be a complete thought. Complete the first two as a group activity.

Example: Julie Priebe won a gold medal in the Olympics. She signed a multi-year contract with the Ice Capades.

If the writer wanted to emphasize that *Julie Priebe won a gold medal in the Olympics,* he could write the following sentence:

Julie Priebe won a gold medal in the Olympics, enabling her to sign a multi-year contract with the Ice Capades.

However, if the writer wanted to emphasize that *Julie Priebe signed a multi-year contract with Ice Capades*, he could write:

After winning a gold medal in the Olympics, **Julie Priebe signed a multi-year contract with the Ice Capades.**

or

Because she won a gold medal in the Olympics, **Julie Priebe signed a multi-year contract with the Ice Capades.**

Although the above sentences seem to be saying the same thing, there is a subtle difference in emphasis in each sentence based on which idea is being stressed. As a good writer, you should be aware of this.

1. McAuley High School has excellent students, and it had many National Merit Scholarship winners this year.

2. The girls' volleyball team lost the game, and they practiced every day for at least three hours.

3. We listened to Tom Aggie's advice. We decided to merge with the other company.

4. Sylvia's mother died. Sylvia was in medical school. She did not become a doctor.

5. The entire team searched for Joshua's contact lens. Darkness came. They did not find them.

6. The old Chevy screeched to a halt, and it disturbed the entire block, and it made plenty of noise.

7. Kevin prepared his camera and his photo lights perfectly. The picture did not turn out well.

8. Alice wanted to become a teacher. She studied hard in high school. She enrolled at Joliet Junior College.

9. The coach made a good basketball player out of the freshman. She taught him to dribble. She taught him to pass. She taught him to shoot. She taught him to play defense.

10. The students clapped. They screamed. They cheered. They stamped their feet. They pounded the steel girders. They added to the tremendous racket.

VARYING SENTENCE LENGTHS

Another technique for emphasizing ideas is to vary sentence lengths. The **Sentence Opening Sheet**, introduced in the **Combining and Rearranging** unit, should have made you aware of the number of words in each of your sentences so that you should be varying your lengths every time you revise your first draft.

Varying sentence lengths enables the writer to avoid the monotony of similar sentence lengths, making it easier for the audience to read the paper. Occasionally writers will write a main idea in a short sentence. The very brevity of the sentence makes the idea stand out in the reader's mind. Here's an excerpt from a student composition dealing with slumlords. Notice how the writer included short sentences to emphasize key ideas.

Slumlords

Their unwitting allies are the courts and the government. Their unwilling victims are the poor, the sick, the aged, and the young. **Their goal is money. They are the slumlords.**

They are ruthless beings who extract millions of dollars a year from the sufferings of others. To get away with it, they put their buildings through a complex legal maze. Money comes out of the maze at one end and the dilapidated, abandoned, or burned buildings come out the other.

Slumlords are slick. They manage to conceal their operations from the public, the courts, the prosecutors, and even their tenants through a smoke screen of confusing transactions, nominees, land trusts, secret deals, phony names, and mysterious operations . . .

EXERCISE 2: On a separate sheet of paper, combine and rearrange the following sentences into one good paragraph. Vary the sentence lengths. Select one or two major ideas and write them in short sentences. Before you begin writing, read the paper aloud to get an overview of the content.

Chaos

1. The bell sounds. **2.** The students are daydreaming. **3.** The students suddenly jump up. **4.** Students are awake. **5.** Students are alert. **6.** Students are energetic. **7.** A feeling of freedom fills the atmosphere. **8.** Books bang shut. **9.** Papers are shoved sloppily into folders. **10.** Everything is hastily stacked. **11.** The stacks are untidy. **12.** Students rejoice wildly. **13.** Students rush up rows. **14.** Students make a direct beeline for the doorway. **15.** The doorway is already jammed. **16.** Students shove. **17.** Students elbow fellow stampeders. **18.** Students try to get through the door. **19.** There are screams of pain. **20.** There are moans of despair. **21.** They come from within the mob. **22.** Victims are angry. **23.** Massive pressure builds up. **24.** There is a break in the jam. **25.** Hassled students stream forth. **26.** They enter an already crowded hallway.

SUMMARY

Subordination is emphasizing a main idea by expressing it as a complete thought in a sentence and subordinating lesser ideas by glue words, WH words, ING words, etc.

One of the keys to becoming a good writer is the ability to express in a clear manner what is important. Learning how to subordinate lesser ideas will help you gain this mastery of the written word.

All of us have a right to believe whatever we want to believe. Often we try to convince others of our opinions, especially opinions that concern us greatly. In this paper you will practice the skill of persuasion so that you can convince your audience to share in your beliefs.

STAGE ONE: PREWRITING

STUDENT LEARNING OBJECTIVES

1. The student will select a controversial issue as his topic.
2. The student will state his opinion in the controlling idea.
3. The student will organize his ideas in an order of importance sequence.
4. The student will support his opinion with specific details.
5. The student will use transition words to indicate the shift from one reason to another.
6. The student will end his persuasive composition by either restating his controlling idea, summarizing the major points, or making a personal comment on the subject.

WRITING PROMPT

In persuasive writing, the writer holds strong feelings about a specific issue and attempts to persuade his audience to agree with his point of view.

Persuasive writing comes in all forms. When you write a business letter of complaint to a company about some product that you bought, are now dissatisfied with, and ask for a refund, that is persuasive writing. When you write a letter to the editor of your school newspaper concerning a controversial issue taking place in your school, that is persuasive writing. When you write an argumentative essay in your social studies class concerning the specific reasons why a certain candidate should be elected, that is persuasive writing.

For this assignment, your subject should be a topic upon which you have strong feelings and can speak with some authority. You must take a stance on one side of a controversial issue and support your position with sound, specific arguments.

It is not enough that you are emotionally charged about your subject. You must be able to support your opinion with good reasons because the audience you are trying to persuade holds beliefs just as deeply as you do about the subject.

One of the dangers in selecting a topic for this assignment is that you might be tempted to choose a current controversial issue, i. e., surrogate motherhood, embargo on Japanese products, English becoming the national language, etc., and run to the library to research your arguments because you do not have adequate personal knowledge to support your position. This is not meant to be a research project unless your teacher directs otherwise. Rather, you should select a topic upon which you have strong feelings and which you can support with personal reasons, observations, examples, facts, etc. Select something that affects you directly.

ROLE-PLAYING

In brainstorming reasons to support your subject, it is important for you to understand your *opponent's* arguments. Role-playing is an excellent prewriting activity to help you "be in the other person's shoes."

EXERCISE 1: Select students and role-play each side of one of the issues.

1. Home schooling has become a controversial issue in many communities throughout the country. Instead of having children attend classes in a school setting, parents are taking them out of the classroom and turning the home into a classroom with the parents serving as teachers.

2. Proposition 48 has caused many exceptional athletes to lose their first year of college eligibility because they did not score high enough on either the SAT or the ACT. As a result, many states are thinking of enacting similar legislation for high school students. If a student does not average "C" in all of his classes, he will be ineligible for **all** extracurricular activities including band, student government, sports, cheerleading, school play, etc.

3. Select a current controversial issue taking place in your community, at your school, or at home. Role-play both sides of the issue. For example, if you wanted to attend a hard rock concert to listen to a new sensational group named *Scott Towel and the Absorbents*, what arguments would you give to your parents so that they would allow you to attend? What arguments would they use against your attending this concert?

SUGGESTED TOPICS

1. Are there any issues that are happening at your home that could be considered for this assignment? Allowance should be raised; curfew should be extended; dating privileges should be expanded; reasons for moving; sister or brother has more freedom; why chores weren't completed on time; privacy in own rooms, i. e., not having to clean them, being allowed to decorate the room, or parents not being allowed to go through drawers, etc.

2. Are there any issues taking place in your school that could be considered controversial? Student lounge for upperclassmen; open campus during lunch periods; smoking area; curriculum changes; discipline code; study halls eliminated; equal use of athletic facilities for boys and girls; home economics classes for everyone, etc.

3. Are there any issues taking place in your classes? Homework on weekends; rules of a specific class; tardiness and attendance policy; student being excused from one class to participate in an activity from another class; grading policy of teachers, etc.

4. Are there any topics related specifically to an issue being discussed in one of your classes?

   PHYSICAL EDUCATION: students involved in a sport should not have to take P. E. during that season; violence in sports; jogging or not jogging; should P. E. be graded or a pass-fail class, etc.

   SOCIAL STUDIES: reasons why an event changed the course of history; prayer in public schools; reasons for or against a political candidate, etc.

   HEALTH: influence of TV on today's youth; relaxation of air pollution standards; craze diets are not healthy; national drinking age raised to 25, etc.

   SCIENCE: use of animals for experimentation; space exploration being worth the money; creationism in science classes, etc.

   MATH: arguments why a student should take an extra math class; boys are better math students than girls, etc.

5. Are there any issues related to your job experience? Hours and pay promises not kept; policy for promotions; promotions being given to owner's family, etc.

6. What controversies are brewing in the sports scene in your community? Should Ed Papulski be fired as the manager of the Appleton Foxes? Is the proposed new sports stadium necessary? Should it be constructed on the west side?

THINK SHEET

Complete the following **Think Sheet** to see if you know enough about your topic to persuade your audience to agree with your point of view. If you cannot supply specific supportive details, do not be afraid to switch topics. That is the purpose of the **Think Sheet**.

As you are completing this **Think Sheet**, you might want to discuss your ideas with a friend or with someone in your cooperative learning group. Remember, talking a topic through is an excellent prewriting strategy.

Also, you might want to make a list of questions that your *opponent* would want to know about your topic.

Name_____

Persuading Think Sheet

1. What is your topic?_____

2. What is your position concerning the topic?_____

    _____

3. List three opposing arguments **against** your position. Be specific.

    a._____

    b._____

    c._____

4. List specific reasons, facts, ideas, examples, and statistics that specifically
    support your position. For each argument provide specific details. No
    assumptions, please.

    a._____

    b._____

    c._____

    d.._____

5. Tentative Controlling Idea_____

    _____

Helpful Hints: Before writing your first draft, organize your ideas in an order of
importance sequence by numbering them on your **Think Sheet**. Number 1 would
be the least important reason and so on. The opposing arguments might be used
as part of your introduction.

CONTROLLING IDEA

In a persuasive essay you are not trying to hide anything from your audience. Therefore, your controlling idea should state the controversial issue and the key words should let your audience know your point of view.

Here are examples of two controlling ideas dealing with the same topic. Which one states the controversial nature of the subject more effectively?

- Little league baseball serves as an excellent source of recreation and personal growth for kids.

- Despite many of today's psychologists believing that little league baseball adds damaging pressure to kids, it serves as an excellent source of recreation and personal growth.

The first statement, barely, if at all, hints at the controversial issue that will be presented in the essay. The second controlling idea recognizes the controversy but still insists on the values of little league baseball.

INTRODUCTORY PARAGRAPH

If you are expected to write an introductory paragraph for this essay, you might want to provide your audience with some background information concerning the issue and then state your controlling idea. It is much easier to write your introduction after you have listed your supportive arguments on your **Think Sheet**. Why? Knowing the content of the body of your essay makes it easier for you to determine how you are going to introduce this information. Here is an example of a background information introductory paragraph:

Background Information

Many consumers only see commercials on TV as ways of selling products and do not really see them as a possible learning experience. Consumers feel that the only thing a commercial does is to remind the viewer over and over again about how good the product is. But there is much more to it than that. Commercials on television do something that no other media can do. They bring necessary education to life in an everyday situation, especially in the areas of economics, history, and futuristics.

Direct Statement of Fact

A direct statement of fact introductory paragraph is another choice for this essay. In this type of introduction you present the opposing side's position and then end with your controlling idea, strongly stating your point of view.

This serves two purposes. First, it disarms your opponent's position. Up front you have presented the arguments against your position. Second, this type of introductory paragraph serves as an excellent way of presenting your view.

ORGANIZING THE PAPER

Your paper should be organized in an order of importance sequence, beginning with the least important argument and ending with the most important. Your strongest argument will be the last idea your audience reads.

Each of your arguments will be the content of a separate developmental paragraph. Each developmental paragraph must include specific supportive information. You must avoid repeating the same ideas over and over again without supplying concrete details. Read the following paragraph from a persuasive essay dealing with war:

> War causes tremendous problems for people all over the world. The problems war causes make it difficult for people to live in peace. These problems are everywhere in the world, the little countries as well as the big ones. Something has to be done about the problems of war.

The student-writer said nothing. He just repeated the same words over and over without supplying specific problems.

GLUING TOGETHER IDEAS

Since you are organizing your essay in an order of importance sequence, you must use transition words that indicate this development.

TRANSITION WORDS FOR ORDER OF IMPORTANCE:
also, another, besides, furthermore, in addition, first, second, next, of primary importance, the least important, the most important, the most appealing, of equal importance, the least, the greatest, etc.

Another way of linking paragraphs is by repeating a key word or idea which smoothly connects the two paragraphs. In the following student example, notice how the writer connects the second paragraph by repeating the phrase *taking advantage of children* and using the transition word *another*.

One shopping center owner, knowing how imitative and impressionable young children are, devised a clever way to give children entering the store small shopping carts. Imitating their parents, the children walked through the store and picked up all types of goodies that interested them. Problems developed, however, when the parent and the child reached the checkout counter. The parent demanded that the child take back all the products that he had put in the cart. When the child resisted and began crying, the parent usually gave in to avoid making a scene.

Another way certain store owners **take advantage of children** is to offer them free gifts if they will bring in their parents to the store. One good example of this is . . .

ENDING

Your conclusion should be part of your overall planning. For this persuasive essay you may restate your controlling idea, summarize all the supporting proofs, make a comment on the issue, or use the weight of your final argument as your last statement.

Since one of the objectives for this persuasive essay is to end with a concluding paragraph, here are some student models:

Finality

Finally, and most importantly, advertising whets the appetites of common people everywhere. In a subtle and spontaneous manner, it bores into the minds of the unschooled in a way that was not possible before the electronic revolution. Advertising has narrowed the gap between the educated and the uneducated.

Economics, history, and futuristics are but three of the variety of subjects to be learned from advertising. All one really has to do is look past the products being offered, and he will have at his disposal a gigantic wealth of information. So next time you are sitting at home watching television and a commercial comes on, don't leave to get food; pay attention to what they are saying. You never know when it might come in handy.

EXERCISE 2: Before writing your first draft, study the sample student composition below. Answer the following questions as a group activity.

1. What is the controlling idea? What is the writer's position?
2. Did the writer include an introductory paragraph? Was it effective? What are some other possible ideas the writer could have used in her introduction?
3. Did the writer organize her ideas in an order of importance sequence?
4. How many arguments did the writer include to support her CI? Are they specific?
5. What other arguments could the writer have used?
6. How did the writer link her ideas?
7. What type of ending did the writer use? Was it effective?

Why I Deserve A Later Curfew

1. Curfew has been a subject of great importance in my home for quite some time now. 2. Arguments between my parents and me are brought up every night at the dinner table. 3. Although 11:30 P.M. is normal curfew for a sixteen-year old, I feel that I deserve a later curfew because of how responsible and trustworthy I am.

4. Being a good student and keeping up all my grades are two of the reasons I deserve a later curfew. 5. Last semester, I was able to maintain a 3.2 grade point average, and was a member of the second honor roll. 6. Working until midnight is something I do quite often on the weekdays, so on the weekends, I should be able to stay out until 12:30 A.M. 7. My working didn't stop me from getting good grades, and I believe that staying out later should be my reward for this.

8. Also, I never get to finish my argument without hearing the famous words, "If your friends were to jump off a building, would you?" 9. My response, of course, is that all of my friends get to stay out later.

10. My parents do have a good answer to this one, and that is: "Your friends are over seventeen years of age, and, by law, they have no curfew." **11.** My argument is that I will be with these kids, who do not have a curfew, and I am more responsible than they are. **12.** My parents do agree with this argument. **13.** They are very much aware that I am a responsible girl, most of the time. **14.** I would never do anything I knew was very wrong, which includes making bad decisions when I am out late with some friends.

15. The last argument is my best one. **16.** I can understand making me come home before curfew If I were roaming the streets at night, but that's not what I'm doing. **17.** I am always in a car, at a particular place, either eating or bowling or doing something to that effect. **18.** Coming home would never be a problem then, because now, my friends have to stop what they're doing, or miss out on doing things because they have to drive me home at 11:30 P.M.

19. I do understand that most girls my age must have a curfew because the law states that they should, but I also feel I personally deserve to stay until 12:30 P.M. instead of 11:30 P.M. **20.** I feel this way because of my maturity when I am out with my friends. **21.** Changing my curfew would make things more convenient for everyone, and I will be very happy. **22.** I just hope I can get my parents to agree with me.

STAGE TWO: WRITING THE FIRST DRAFT

Write your first draft with your completed **Think Sheet** in front of you. Skip every other line and number your sentences. Here is a brief review of the objectives for this assignment:

1. Your controlling idea should let your audience know your opinion.
2. If you are expected to write an introductory paragraph, background information or opposing view arguments are two possible options.
3. Your paper should be organized in an order of importance sequence.
4. Each argument needs specific, supportive details. If your arguments are not specific, expand by using the journalistic questions studied in **Unit 3**.
5. Use order of importance transition words to indicate which ideas you consider to be important.
6. End your paper with a sense of finality. Recapping the controlling idea, summarizing, or making a personal comment are all possibilities.

Now write the first draft.

STAGE THREE: REWRITING

SENTENCE OPENING SHEET

With your first draft completed, fill out your **Sentence Opening Sheet**.

Column One   **First Four Words Per Sentence**

1. Do all of my sentences begin with the same word or structure?
2. Can I combine or rearrange my sentences to make them more interesting?

Column Two   **Special (Teacher Pet Peeve)**

1. Did I use transition words to shift from one argument to the next?

Column Three   **Verbs**

1. Are all my verbs in the same tense? Did I repeat the same weak verbs?
2. Could I substitute more concrete verbs for the weak verbs?

Column Four   **Number of Words Per Sentence**

1. Did I use any short sentences to emphasize a particular idea?
2. Are any of my overly long sentences run-ons?
3. Can I combine any of my short, choppy sentences to make them more interesting?

PEER EVALUATION USING A CHECKLIST SHEET

In checking over your partner's composition, make sure that he adhered to the objectives as stated in the **Student Learning Objectives** at the beginning of this unit.

If any of the arguments seem unclear and need more information, expand by providing some of your own ideas. Do not just identify mistakes. Help your partner correct them. Treat his paper as if it were your own. No assumptions.

Persuading Checklist Sheet

1. Did the writer clearly state her point of view about the topic in the controlling idea?

2. If the writer introduced her controlling idea with an introductory paragraph, did the introduction peak your interest? In other words, did you want to find out more about the issue?

3. Did the writer organize her ideas in an order of importance sequence?

4. Is each argument fully developed? Did the writer's arguments convince you to share in her opinion? Why or why not?

5. Circle all the transition words and repeated phrases on the first draft that indicate the shift from one argument to another.

6. Did the paper end with a sense of finality? Was the ending effective? If not, why?

7. What one suggestion would you make for the writer to improve the paper?

STAGE FOUR: PUBLISHING

Some volunteers might share their persuasive essay by reading them aloud to the class. Then the class can argue whether the supportive statements were valid.

Also, you might want to have the individual who disagrees with your opinion read your final draft. Maybe your persuasive points will change his/her point of view.

You might also want to send your persuasive essay to either the local newspaper or your school newspaper.

Finally, you might want to include this piece in your writing portfolio.

In **Unit 14** you emphasized main thoughts by **subordinating** lesser ideas. You introduced these lesser ideas with subordinating conjunctions (glue words), present participles and gerunds (ING words), and past participles (ED words). Now you will concentrate on **coordinating** ideas to show equal value.

PARALLEL STRUCTURES

Nouns: The sports area included **perfectly manicured baseball diamonds, a half dozen tennis courts, two spacious soccer fields, two handball areas,** <u>and</u> **a number of basketball hoops.**

Verbs: Kicking the competition into gear, the sophomores **stamped** their feet, **threw** confetti, <u>and</u> **yelled** out their familiar cheer, "Harass them. Harass them. Make them relinquish the ball."

Gerunds: **Collecting** stamps <u>and</u> **saving** old coins are favorite hobbies for young children.

Present Participles: Sal Kozinski ran in front of the class, **waving** his arms, **blowing** his whistle, <u>and</u> **shouting** at the top of his lungs.

Prepositional Phrases: Candy Millrose scattered her clothes **on the floor, on top of the bed,** <u>and</u> **under the dresser.**

Relative Pronouns: The old Slovak lady, **who washes walls, (**who**) scrubs wooden floors on her knees,** <u>and</u> **(**who**) uses an old board to clean clothes,** owns twelve apartment buildings on Michigan Avenue.

You have practiced using glue words (subordinating conjunctions) to introduce subordinate ideas. Here are glue words (coordinating conjunctions) that connect equal ideas. Just remember the expression **BOYS FAN**.

But .... contrast
Or .... option
Yet .... contrast
So .... result

For .... alternative
And .... addition
Nor .... negation

A few conjunctions are used in pairs. They are called correlative conjunctions: *not only . . . but also; either . . . or; neither . . . nor; both . . . and; whether . . . or.*

- **Not only** did Alex Dogoodie win the spelling bee **but (also)** he received $6,000,000 from the event's sponsor, Kamakazi of Japan.

- **Either** Uncle Wally **or** Uncle Dickie is the most handsome relative in the Hrebic family, according to them.

- **Neither** Theresa **nor** Elsie will wait for anyone to give the answer.

- **Both** the piano **and** the TV were dropped by Nobreak Movers, Inc.

- **Whether** Mrs. Shapulski **or** Mrs. Rodriguez gets the job will be determined in the next few days.

EXERCISE 1: Combine the following sentences by using glue words (coordinating conjunctions = **BOYS FAN**) that connect equal ideas.

Example: Sophie examined the diamonds. She did not buy any.
Rewritten: Sophie examined the diamonds, **but** she did not buy any.

1. I will go to the party.
   I won't dance the boogaloo with Oscar Hemkin.

2. My name was called to recite the poem.
   I ran up the aisle.

3. German shepherds are faster runners than collies.
   Collies are gentlier with children.

4. Sarah was fatter and more muscular than Olen.
   He let her carry him over the threshold.

5. Riding my Lifecycle at home allows me to trim down.
   It enables me to exercise at home instead of going to the health club.

6. The Corvette broke down twice.
   It won the race.

7. I had an opportunity to buy a go-kart.
   I bought a dune buggy.

8. The girls were given five detentions each.
   They had put peanut butter in Myron's hair.

EXERCISE 2: Combine the following sentences into one by first subtracting the repeated pronouns and then combining by using a series of verbs.

Example: Peppy Pringle **pried** open the can of paint. **He mixed** the paint with a stirring stick. **He poured** the paint into a roller pan.

Rewritten: Peppy Pringle **pried** open the can of paint, **mixed** the paint with a stirring stick, <u>and</u> **poured** the paint into a roller pan.

1. Hector sat down to the table.
   He forked a two pound potato.
   He sliced it in half.
   He gulped both pieces down with one swallow.

2. Millie filled the bucket with hot water.
   She poured in a capful of Mr. Clean.
   She plopped her mop into the bucket.

3. Jorge lumbered to the counter.
   He planted himself firmly on the stool.
   He ordered 24 White Castle Hamburgers for a light snack.

4. Sylvester strutted down the boulevard.
   He tipped his derby to the young ladies on the corner.
   He lit up a Cuban cigar.

5. The students rushed out of the class.
   They banged their heads on the entrance.
   They stampeded down the corridor like a herd of wild monkeys.

EXERCISE 3: Combine the following sentences into one by using ING words, glue words, and/or WH words to coordinate equal ideas.

Example: Wanda stomped her feet. She clapped her hands. She jumped up and down. She kept warm.

Rewritten: By **stomping** her feet, **clapping** her hands, <u>and</u> **jumping** up and down, Wanda kept warm. **(ING Words)**

Because Wanda stomped her feet, clapped her hands, <u>and</u> jumped up and down, Wanda kept warm. **(Glue Word)**

Wanda, **who** stomped her feet, clapped her hands, and jumped up <u>and</u> down, kept warm. **(WH Words)**

1. Casey Kismadski closed his eyes.
   He puckered his lips.
   He leaned forward.
   He planted a smooch on Gretchen's tender cheek.

2. The torrential downpour saturated the dried fields.
   It smashed down the vegetation.
   It flooded the dry creek.

3. The team bus spun out of control.
   It careened off the guard rail.
   It smashed into an oncoming truck.

4. People who work in downtown Manhattan come to work in various ways.
   Some ride cars.
   Some take buses.
   Some ride cabs.
   Some use the subway.

5. Brigid boiled the potatoes.
   She sliced the corned beef.
   She garnished the salad.

EXERCISE 4: On a separate sheet of paper, expand each sentence with an equal idea. Be imaginative.

Example: Either by working overtime or by_____,
                 Charlotte will be able to buy a new car.

Expanded: Either by working overtime or by *borrowing from the bank*,
                 Charlotte will be able to buy a new car.

1. Either by scoring three goals **or** by _____,
   a soccer fullback will receive praise from Coach Marty Mongan.

2. The diver will immediately perform **or** _____.

3. Cousin Wally's interests center around UPS **and** _____.

4. Leo picked up the bat, walked up to the plate, **and** _____.

5. Chelsea's handwriting proved to be neat, _____, **and**
   _____.

6. The dancer twirled on the mat **and** _____.

7. A fly buzz**ing** in the room, _____ **and** _____ landed on Herman's nose.

8. _____ , _____**and** to be trustworthy are the requirements of a team captain.

9. Patti proposed that we fly a kite, _____ _____, **and** _____ before we take our lunch break.

10. Whether Paul decides to enroll at John Marshall Law School **or** _____ , will be determined in the new few days.

EXERCISE 5: When writing a series of balanced ideas, make sure the ideas follow a logical sequence. You can organize your equal ideas in an order of importance sequence, a chronological sequence, or a spatial sequence. Rearrange the following ideas in a logical sequence. Be able to defend your organization.

Example: He saves nickels, pennies, and dimes.

Rewritten: He saves pennies, nickels, and dimes.

1. To not to be or to be: that is the question.

2. From the moment the game ends until it begins, the players must use their wits to outsmart and outmaneuver their opponents.

3. Constance climbed to the top of the ladder, dove, and approached the end of the diving board.

4. Composition students must apply and remember every writing technique to help themselves in writing good papers.

5. Casper pulled out the plug, the clean hot water went down the drain, and he jumped into the tub to take a shower.

FAULTY PARALLELISM

Probably the most difficult error for students to identify and to correct is faulty parallelism in sentences. Faulty parallelism occurs when the writer uses coordinating conjunctions and correlative conjunctions (special equal idea glue words) to connect ideas, but does not use equal structures. In other words, instead of connecting a noun with a noun he connects a noun with a phrase or clause.

Example: Aristotle Savalas is a sophomore **with a bright mind** <u>and</u> **who has high principles.**

In the example, the writer used the glue word *and* to connect **with a bright mind** and **who has high principles**. These structures are not equal.

Rewritten: Aristotle Savalas is a sophomore **with a bright mind** <u>and</u> **with high principles.**

Example: **Jogging** <u>and</u> **to swim** are great ways to lose weight.

Rewritten: **Jogging** <u>and</u> **swimming** are great ways to lose weight.

EXERCISE 6: Rewrite the following sentences on a separate sheet of paper, correcting the faulty parallelism. Complete the first two as a group activity.

1. Yogi Gavelda spends all of his time organizing bowling tournaments and to practice his putting in golf.

2. The secretary must attend all the meetings, call the roll, and keeping notes.

3. To sail a small boat and driving a pontoon boat require different skills.

4. Not only did Grace excel in Spanish but also doing well in Polish.

5. Her duties are cleaning up the office and to organize a pep rally for Friday's game against Brother Rice High School.

6. Students fall naturally into two classes: the hard workers and those who delay doing their homework until the last moment.

7. General Zigmond asked why the soldiers were playing cards and not cleaned up the barracks.

8. Ms. Childs said that she would give us a quiz on Monday and for us to study the first two chapters of the book.

9. Both the chefs in the cafeteria and those who prepare salads in the kitchen went on strike.

10. Stefanie's serious manner and the fact that she lacked any outward sign of emotion caused worry on the part of her counselors and those who teach her.

SUMMARY

Parallel structures enable the writer to emphasize equal ideas through equal structures. This balance lends a smoothness and harmony to the writing.

Remember, when ideas are equal in your mind, express them in the same structure.

One of the best ways we learn about new people and new things is by comparing and/or contrasting them to people and things we already know. We examine the similarities and the differences and gain new insights.

The organization of a comparison-contrast paper is one that you will be using in many of your academic classes, especially in literature and social studies writing assignments. It is a pattern that will help you organize your essay exam answers that deal with comparison-contrast topics.

STAGE ONE: PREWRITING

STUDENT LEARNING OBJECTIVES

1. The student will state the two topics being written about in the controlling idea and indicate the direction of the paper.
2. The student will organize the ideas using either the block method, the flip-flop method, or a combination of the two.
3. The student will supply specific supportive details with each topic.
4. The student will use transition words to point out similarities or differences or repeat key phrases or structures.
5. The student will end the paper with a sense of finality, possibly summarizing the major points or commenting on the major idea proven in the paper.

WRITING PROMPT

The topics that you select for this **Comparing--Contrasting** paper should come from your personal experiences or from a writing across the curriculum assignment (student model p.146) given by one of your teachers in your other academic classes. Whatever topics you select, it is important that you know them thoroughly so that you can support your ideas with specific details.

Also, it is important that you have balance to your ideas. It is not enough that you know one of your topics well and just mention that the second topic is similar or different. Your supportive ideas must be specific and balanced for both topics.

EXERCISE 1: The **Suburban and Urban Living** composition is *what not to do* in your writing. Read it and complete a **T-bar Think Sheet** similar to the one on page 142 on a separate sheet of paper. Then discuss the following questions:

1. What are the two subjects being written about?
2. What is their common element?
3. Does the writer supply an equal number of ideas for each topic?
4. Which ideas are not specific enough and need to be expanded?

Suburban and Urban Living

1. It is interesting to compare the living conditions of suburban people and people who live in the city. **2.** The income of suburbanites ranges from middle to high. **3.** Their reasons for moving away from the city vary, but the three most important facts are pollution, overcrowded stores and expressways, and lousy neighbors and poor school buildings. **4.** Suburban living contains none of these problems. **5.** For the city people many of the problems of suburbanites attract them to the city. **6.** Stores are much more convenient. **7.** Transportation systems are everywhere. **8.** The income of the city people ranges from low to high. **9.** The people are as different as their incomes. **10.** For a city person found it a challenge to experience a variety of cultures and going to the many places a big city offers. **11.** What is the bad element for one man is the good for the other. **12.** Only the individual must decide what he wants.

NARROWING TOPICS

You have freedom of choice to select any two topics to compare and/or contrast as long as you know them well. In fact, you might want to practice the persuasion skills you have learned by writing about two products and showing why one is better or superior to the other.

Obviously, the writer of the **Suburban and Urban Living** composition needed to narrow down his general subjects. He failed to support his ideas with specific details. He just listed superficial information. He wrote a classic "So What" composition.

139

You must also decide whether you are going to write about the similarities or the differences of your two subjects or possibly both. Even though you are free to choose your own topic, it might be easier to write about subjects that on the surface appear to be quite similar. Your main purpose, then, would be to find the major differences between the subjects selected.

SUGGESTED TOPICS

As a group, discuss some of the suggested topics, always narrowing down the ideas to make them more personal and specific for you. Select one common topic that everyone can brainstorm about, e. g., two products that everyone in the class uses. Or how about two students' volunteering to stand in front of the class and having the class brainstorm their career--goals, attitude towards school, athletic abilities, etc.

1. People: two brothers; two sisters; two teachers; two friends; two grandparents; two neighbors, etc.

2. Celebrities: movie stars; football heroes; disc jockeys; musical groups, etc.

3. TV and radio programs: two shows with same format, i.e., situation comedy; two favorite movies, etc.

4. Products: cosmetics; toilet bowl cleaners; fast food restaurants, i. e., Wendy's vs. McDonald's; cars, etc.

5. Facilities: athletic facilities of two schools; two rooms that you have lived in; before and after room (remodeling), etc.

6. Recreation and vacation: amusement parks; reaction to two vacations, etc.

7. Hobbies: skills of two sports; skills of two hobbies, etc.

8. Writing Across the Curriculum:
   a. Social Studies: two cultures; two political figures; etc.
   b. Home Economics: two ways of cooking fish, etc.
   c. Art: two artists; two styles of art, etc.
   d. Shop: two types of wood; two tools; uses of computers, etc.
   e. Foreign Language: two cultures; contrasting the teaching styles of two foreign language teachers, etc.
   f. Literature: two characters from the same play, novel, or short story. See the *Julius Caesar* and *Black Boy* units later in *Stack*.

THINK SHEET

Once you have selected your two subjects, jot down all of your ideas using a **T-bar Think Sheet**. When you write down an idea for your first topic, jot down a corresponding idea for the second one.

Be specific with each idea. For example, a student in a home economics class was writing a comparison--contrast paper on the advantages of microwave ovens over regular ovens. Here are some of the ideas he included on his **T-bar Think Sheet.**

1. What are the two items being compared and/or contrasted?

    A. Microwave oven   B. Regular oven

2. What is their common element?
    Both are used to cook food.

3. Jot down specific ideas for each item being compared or contrasted.

    A. Microwave Oven   B. Regular Oven

    1. Time saving   1. Time losing
        Cooks a roast in 30 minutes   Cooks a roast in 3 hours

    2. No preheating   2. Preheating oven
        No 15 minute wait   Need to warm up oven
        Put food right in   Waste gas heating up
        Keeps kitchen cool,   Hot kitchen all the time
            especially in summer

    3 . Defrosting faster   3. Must leave meat out
        No need to wait for hours   Possible bacteria
        Plan more meals around   Can't prepare last minute
            frozen food   meals

What other ideas might he have included?

After your **T-bar Think Sheet** is completed, you might want to exchange it with a fellow student. In fact, your teacher might ask for some of you to volunteer your **Think Sheets** to be duplicated or put on transparencies for class discussion. In jotting down ideas, try to list three or four major divisions which will serve as the main topics for each of your developmental paragraphs.

Name_____Period_____

Comparing--Contrasting Think Sheet

1.   What are the two subjects being compared or contrasted?

   A. _____   B. _____

2.   What is their common element? _____

   _____

3.   Jot down specific ideas for each subject being compared or contrasted.

   1. _____   _____

   2. _____   _____

   3. _____   _____

   4. _____   _____

   5. _____   _____

   6. _____   _____

   7. _____   _____

   8. _____   _____

   9. _____   _____

   10. _____   _____

Tentative controlling idea _____

_____

_____

Special Hint: Make your ideas specific. Do not include general and vague words like *kind*, *good*, *tall*, *responsible*, etc. Expand when necessary.

CONTROLLING IDEA

Now that you have completed your **T-bar Think Sheet**, you are ready to begin writing your first draft. Your controlling idea should mention the two topics being compared and/or contrasted. The key words should indicate your point of view on the subject. In other words, your audience should know if you are going to write a comparison or a contrast paper. They should also know if you favor one of your topics over the other.

If you are writing a multi-paragraph composition, your controlling idea should be part of your introductory paragraph. The purpose of the introductory paragraph is to peak your reader's interest and indicate the direction your paper will take.

Here are examples of introductory paragraphs:

The Moods of Winter---New York and Miami

As the blanket of winter envelops the nation, the moods it produces are as varied as snowflakes or grains of sand. There are moods to suit the tastes of the sun-worshipper as well as those of the snow bunny. **Although winter comes at the same time to New Yorkers   and Miamians, the separation of I,000 miles makes a distinct difference in the winter lifestyles of these people.**

Chores! Yuk!

Of all the household chores that my parents make me do to collect my measly $1.50 weekly allowance, cleaning the bathroom toilet bowl is the most repulsive. I shiver whenever I think about it. Fortunately, they allow me to use any product that will make my job easier. **After much experimentation, I have discovered that Ty-D-Bowl Cleaner   is far superior to Vanish.**

ORGANIZING THE PAPER

One way of organizing your ideas is to write all of your information on the first topic and then all the information on the second one. This is called the **block method.** This organizational pattern is used if you want your audience to see the total picture of each of your topics.

Another method of organization is the **flip-flop method**. First, you write one specific idea about your first topic and then a corresponding idea about the second one. This lends itself to a point by point analysis. In using the **flip-flop method**, remember that your audience must read through all the information about your second topic, stop, and try to remember how this second one compares to the first.

Either of these organizational patterns may be used or a combination of them. However, before writing your first draft, decide upon which method suits your purpose.

Each paragraph should concentrate on one major element and include specific supportive details. For example, if the purpose of your paper was to prove to your audience that the Dodge Caravan is superior to the Ford Aerostar, one of your developmental paragraphs might deal with the comforts of each car. You would need to describe the special comforts of each vehicle and show how the Caravan's are superior to the Aerostar's.

Your other paragraphs might cover each car's performance and handling or the cost of each car, including the options. It is much easier to think of accomplishing short term goals than of reaching a specific number of words.

GLUING TOGETHER IDEAS

In linking ideas for this composition, use transition words that point out similarities and differences. Here are some of these words:

TRANSITION WORDS (GLUE) FOR SIMILARITIES:
similarly, likewise, in the same manner, equally, in a similar fashion, etc.

TRANSITION WORDS (GLUE) FOR DIFFERENCES:
yet, still, but, although, however, rather, on the contrary, whereas, despite, nevertheless, on the other hand, instead of, etc.

Another way of gluing together ideas is to repeat similar patterns or key phrases. This technique not only links ideas but also creates impact through the repetition of the key words. Here's an example from a student paper dealing with the similarities of early American pioneers and modern day astronauts:

In the pioneer days the settlers, trekking across the Middle West and onto deserts and mountains, faced dangers of **unknown** invaders, which ranged from Indians to rustlers, **unknown** territory, which spread across thousands of unexplored miles, and **unknown** land dangers, which ranged from landslides to broken axles.

In the atomic age the astronauts, rocketing across the universe and onto the moon and other planets, face the perils of **mysterious** invaders, which include solar rays and interterrestial gases, **mysterious** territory, which reaches across the vast expanse of unexplored areas, and **mysterious** space dangers, which vary from meteor showers to mechanical malfunctions.

ENDING

Your composition cannot just end without your audience feeling satisfied that you have completed your assignment. For this organizational pattern you may want to provide a short recap or summary.

Another effective conclusion is to end with the last major point as long as you provide the transition words that let your audience know that your paper is over. You may also want to end by making some personal commentary about your subjects. Here are two examples:

American Explorers: Pioneers and Astronauts

Finally, an individual with a certain amount of curiosity, daring, and adventure becomes the explorer. In the pioneer and the astronaut, one finds a personality that seeks a new way, a sense of freedom, a bit of adventure. Not just any man would leave his secure little home and possessions to journey on a perilous trip to a distant and dangerous territory. Not just any man would risk his life and go speeding through space in a tiny space capsule to an unexplored and airless moon. Not just any man has.

Brains, Not Muscles

Although an athlete's physical prowess or brawn plays a major role in sports, her intelligence and ability to apply her talents successfully should not be outweighed by this. The athlete's intelligence ensures the success or the failure of any game. It's the brain that counts.

STUDENT MODEL

Before you begin to write your first draft, read the following student composition. An art student selected this topic as a writing across the curriculum assignment. Use the **Checklist Sheet** questions on page 149 as your guide.

America's Artists

(A) Two of the most popular American artists of the twentieth century are Norman Rockwell and Leroy Neiman. The works of these men can be found not only in art galleries and exhibits throughout the country, but also in the homes of private collectors. Even ad agencies on Madison Avenue use their paintings to portray different segments of American life in commercials and ads on television and on the printed page. Norman Rockwell and Leroy Neiman have achieved this widespread popularity despite drastic differences in the way they approach art.

(B) Norman Rockwell has long been associated with realism. His works are literal, and at times almost photographic. Rockwell paints with intricate detail, yet his works retain their aura of simplicity. He paints of simple life, a life with which everyone can identify. He paints of Thanksgiving dinner, Mom's cooking, children playing, and encounters with Santa Claus. He brings to mind fond memories of times gone by, an ability which accounts for his universal appeal.

(C) Neiman's style differs drastically from that of Rockwell's. Often Neiman's style borders on the abstract or even surreal, a product of his great admiration for Salvador Dali. Neiman holds little interest in detail. He paints in a very general manner, and often, one may have a difficult time seeing what is on one of his canvases. Yet when one is told what is in the painting, the once random and confused patches of color seem to come alive, and like a whirlwind of rainbow colored leaves, they flurry about and then settle down to reveal the true form of the subjects being painted.

(D) Rockwell's paintings are modest, straightforward, and honest. By reading the expressions of the faces of his characters, one can easily see what situation or story his work is presenting. Rockwell also employs familiarity in his characters as well as in the situations he portrays. If one looks closely at the soda jerk in one of his works, for example, the soda jerk appears to be the spitting image of the red-haired, freckle-faced kid next door.

(E) Neiman's subjects are also in contrast to Rockwell. Neiman's paintings are primarily of night life and various sporting scenes. Perhaps because of his association with *Playboy* magazine, Neiman spends much of his time sketching and painting countless night clubs, gambling casinos, bars, and, of course, ladies. He also paints the world of athletics, from the long, grueling matches between boxers, to the swift, two minute runs of the sport of kings: horse racing.

(F) Because of his commitment to realism, Rockwell uses dull or subdued colors in his paintings. These colors do not detract from his pictures, however. The plainness of the colors lends a casual, down-home feeling to his scenes.

(G) These scenes, whether there is movement represented or not, always seem to remain in photographic stillness. It is almost as though he paints in the same way a camera takes a picture, providing us with a still-life slice of life in America. Perhaps this is the simple most important reason for Rockwell's popularity. His paintings portray for us the simple pleasures and ideals of our everyday lives that are so dear in our hearts.

(H) In contrast to Rockwell's colors, Neiman's paintings, no matter what the topic, are always a virtual kaleidoscope of flying, dancing, bustling colors. They provide a great deal of movement and fluidity to his canvases. Just as one can almost hear the clinking of glasses and steady drone of conversation in a Neiman night club painting, so one can feel the muscles straining and the adrenaline pumping through the bodies of sleek thoroughbreds, thundering down the racetrack.

(I) Neiman's world is a world of both the great, and those who wish to be great; the winners and the losers, the gaudy nouveau rich and the quiet, stately wealth of established millionaires.

(J) His paintings present to us both "life in the fast lane" and "the live-fast-die-young" lifestyles of those seeking instant gratification, and the long term dedication of athletes seeking physical perfection.

(K) Despite their apparent differences, Normal Rockwell and Leroy Neiman do share the common accomplishments of widespread recognition and acceptance. This acceptance is proof that there is room for creativity and originality in popular art and that the American public has a lot more artistic understanding and appreciation than they are given credit for.

STAGE TWO: WRITING THE FIRST DRAFT

With your **Think Sheet** completed, write your first draft. Follow the same procedure that you have been doing up to now. Skip every other line and number your sentences.

Here is a brief review of the objectives for this assignment:

1. Peak your audience's interest in your opening. Let them know your two subjects and the point of view of your paper.
2. Organize your ideas in either the block method, the flip-flop method or a combination of the two.
3. Support your subjects with specific details in each developmental paragraph.
4. Use appropriate transition words to point out similarities or differences and to tie ideas together within and between paragraphs.
5. End with a sense of finality. Let your audience know your feelings about your subjects.

Now write the first draft.

STAGE THREE: REWRITING

SENTENCE OPENING SHEET

Complete the **Sentence Opening Sheet** as directed by your teacher. Use the guidelines from pages 13-15.

PEER EVALUATION USING A CHECKLIST SHEET

Exchange first drafts with your proofreading partner. Read his paper two or three times so that you understand the content before you begin marking up the paper. Use the questions from the **Checklist Sheet** as your guide.

Treat your partner's paper as if it were your own.

Writer's Name_____

Corrector's Name_____

Comparing--Contrasting Checklist Sheet

l. Does the writer mention the two subjects in the controlling idea and the point of view of the paper?

2. Does the introduction peak your interest so that you want to continue reading? If not, what could the writer add to make the introduction more interesting?

3. What organizational pattern did the writer use? Block? Flip-Flop? Combination? Does the pattern used give you a good understanding of the two topics?

4. Does the writer supply specific supportive details for each idea he is using? If not, identify the weak areas on the first draft and offer some expansion suggestions.

5. How did the writer glue together his ideas? Transition words? Repeated phrases?

6. What type of ending did the writer use? Did he summarize or comment on his position?

7. What one suggestion would you make for the writer to improve the comparison--contrast?

STAGE FOUR: PUBLISHING

A comparison--contrast paper is an ideal one for an oral report or speech.

Also, if some classmates have written on similar topics, e. g., products, environmental issues, you might want to compile them in a book format.
Or you might want to exchange papers to see how they handle the same topics.

Finally, you might want to include your paper in a writing portfolio.

First and Last

During your remaining English classes you undoubtedly will be required to write many multi-paragraph literary analysis compositions in response to your study of the novel, the short story, the play, or the poem. Consequently, various types of introductory and concluding paragraphs, written by students, are presented here to serve as models and to help you in writing your own introductory and concluding paragraphs.

We suggest that you write your introductory paragraph after you have jotted down ideas on your **Think Sheet** and have written the developmental paragraphs for your paper. By following this order, you will have a much easier time in writing your introductory paragraph since you will know the content of the body and the sequence in which it is organized. After writing a number of multi-paragraph compositions following this pattern, if you feel it is easier to write the introductory paragraph first before you write the body of your paper, go ahead.

Remember, the purposes of introductory paragraphs are: 1) to introduce the subject of your paper; 2) to excite your audience to read on; 3) to indicate the direction of your paper.

Writing a concluding paragraph is probably the most difficult part in writing a multi-paragraph composition. All too frequently students spend so much time writing their introductory and developmental paragraphs, that they tend to write their concluding paragraph without taking the necessary time to plan a good conclusion to their paper. This is a mistake. Remember, your concluding paragraph will include the last ideas your audience will read. Therefore, spend time working on your concluding paragraph so that your reader has a clear understanding of what you have accomplished in your paper and senses the finality of your last thoughts.

Study the following student introductory and concluding paragraphs. Refer to this unit every time you are required to write introductory and concluding paragraphs for literary analysis papers.

INTRODUCTORY PARAGRAPHS

Background Information Introductory Paragraph

A background information introductory paragraph supplies the reader with information that he/she might not be familiar with. It enables the writer to point out significant facts about the story so that the reader has some general idea concerning the topic.

In his play, ***The Caine Mutiny Court Martial***, Herman Wouk presented the story of a young naval lieutenant being tried for the mutinous act of relieving his commanding officer. Lt. Steve Maryk, the accused, was a young man with only a few year's experience in the Navy, whereas his commanding officer, Lt. Commander Philip Francis Queeg, possessed an unblemished record of fourteen years of military service. As the play progressed, tension rose as the defense attorney and judge advocate pitted the credibility of Maryk against that of Queeg. Under such a stress-filled situation, many facets of Commander Queeg's character were revealed. His dominant traits, background, inner feelings and emotions, as well as questionable personal integrity were exposed through his interaction with other characters.

Examples Introductory Paragraph

The use of an example or examples to concretize a generality enables the reader to gain an understanding of the topic. It provides the reader with a point of comparison.

Man displays a desire to live at the expense of others. He will sit on a bus or walk down a street and see someone being brutally attacked by muggers, and he will turn his head the other way. He will read the daily newspaper headlines of murders in his own city, and he will think nothing of it as long as it doesn't touch his family. He will read the statistics of over 40,000 people being killed each year in car accidents on our nation's highways, yet he will still have that last martini or beer and ignore the speed limit as he weaves his way down the highway. In fact, in primitive times man even sacrificed the life of another human being for a god he was never sure existed so that his life would be safe. Shirley Jackson's short story, "The Lottery," captured man caring only for himself. The characters in the story clearly demonstrated the instinct of self preservation.

A Direct Statement of Fact Introductory Paragraph

Similar to a background information introductory paragraph, a direct statement of fact introductory paragraph immediately explains exactly what will be proven in the paper.

In the play ***The Tragedy of Julius Caesar*** by William Shakespeare, two differing speeches concerning Caesar's death were given. One, by Marcus Brutus, appealed to the intellect of the crowd, stating simply and directly that Caesar was killed for the betterment of Rome and that the conspirators were justified in his assassination. Antony, on the other hand, appealed to the emotions of the crowd and employed a variety of strategic gimmicks, implying indirectly that Caesar's assassination was murder, that Caesar was a good man, and that the traitors should pay for their crime. While Brutus tried to calm and settle down the crowd, Antony succeeded in stirring up anger and revenge in the crowd, turning the people into a blood thirsty mob.

Here is another example of a direct statement of fact introduction:

The nameless man in Jack London's "To Build a Fire" decided to challenge the back roads of the Yukon trail, not realizing that he would face nature at its worst. This man made numerous mistakes before and during his journey which caused him to meet his fate--a frigid death.

An Incident Introductory Paragraph

An incident provides a dramatic background before the controlling idea by providing the reader with a story that captures his/her interest. If you select this type of introductory paragraph, make sure that your incident relates to the idea you are illustrating and that you include some statement that ties the incident to your subject.

After receiving his daily ration of bread, Ivan Denisovich lifted it, turned it and looked at it in the same way as he had done thousands of times before. Many of the other men did the same thing hoping that maybe this time they received their full ration of bread for the day. Although they realized they had no way of knowing if they received their full pound, they did it only to put their minds at ease. The author of the book ***One Day in the Life of Ivan Denisovich***, Alexander Solzhenitsyn, used such tonal passages to bring forth a mood of hopelessness and monotony.

Comparison Introductory Paragraph

In writing a comparison introductory paragraph, make sure the relationship between your two items is clear to your reader. This type of introductory paragraph is often used when the subject is technical or highly sophisticated. The comparison is used to make the complex subject clear to the reader. In many cases objects from nature are used.

In the world of nature, life progresses in a well-balanced manner. Each individual serves a definite purpose corresponding with another individual. This form of life can be compared with a chain, each link, equally as important for the chain's strength, having a single flaw which sets it apart from all others. In nature a change or mutant becomes an accepted part of the "nature chain" quite easily. The new "changed" member may be considered an asset or an improvement to nature itself. The new member may be considered the highly cast link in the improvement of the "chain's" durability and strength. Although this seems the ideal life style, the nature of man appears the direct opposite. The "change" or mutant, regardless of the personal qualities he may possess, becomes a "disdained, disgusting, and degradable oddity" who weakens life's chain. When viewed in this light, the nature of man becomes evil and corrupt in the face of change. Through the development of various characters in the novel *Flowers for Algernon*, Daniel Keyes, the author, shows an ideal view of the evil and corruption of man's nature.

Quotation Introductory Paragraph

Just as a quotation can be an effective concluding paragraph, it also can be an effective introductory paragraph. However, you must make sure the quotation relates directly to the subject of your paper and comes from a reliable source. It is not sufficient just to begin the introduction with a quotation. You must also blend in the quotation with the purpose and subject of your paper.

"The whites had drawn a line over which we dared not step and we accepted that line because our bread was at stake. But within our boundaries we, too, drew a line that included our right to bread regardless of the indignities or degradations involved in getting it." Richard Wright in his autobiography *Black Boy* explained through this statement the pain and hardships shared by all Southern Negroes of that era. He was surrounded on the one side by Negroes who resented anyone trying to rise above the common lot and on the other by whites who were indifferent to him, pitying, or cruel. Both of these groups contributed to his eventual escape to the North and his rebellion against both types of oppression.

A Definition Introductory Paragraph

A definition introductory paragraph is another effective way to introduce the subject of your paper.

A short story, which is a brief fictional narrative written in prose, is composed of four basic elements: plot, setting, character, and theme. The author of a good short story skillfully blends these elements to produce a lasting single effect on the reader. Richard Connell accomplished this in his short story "The Most Dangerous Game." By blending plot, setting, and character, Richard Connell has managed to leave the reader with a feeling of mystery by requiring the involvement of the reader's imagination in many parts of the story.

CONCLUDING PARAGRAPHS

Summarization Concluding Paragraph

The most commonly used concluding paragraph is summarization. The writer simply repeats the main ideas from the developmental paragraphs. This serves to reinforce the supportive statements and leaves the reader with a lasting impression of the purpose of the paper.

Herman Wouk used all his skills as a playwright in his gradual but thorough revelation of Lt. Commander Queeg's character. First, Queeg's general personality traits were brought out through his testimony in court and accounts of his behavior while aboard ship. Second, Queeg's inner turmoil was gradually revealed through testimony attributing to his unblemished record, and also through changes in Queeg's manner and emotional bearing as the trial tactics used against him became more intense. Third, Wouk provided an explanation for Queeg's paranoia by explaining his background through the testimony of Dr. Lundeen. The revelation of all these traits culminated when Queeg broke down before the court and rattled on and on, attempting to rationalize his behavior. In this gradual revelation of Queeg through his interaction with other characters, Wouk developed the personality of Lt. Commander Queeg to its fullest in *The Caine Mutiny Court Martial.*

155

Here is another example from a student paper dealing with Shirley Jackson's "The Lottery":

> All of these examples proved that the characters cared only for themselves. This attitude could be felt in the silence of the crowd when the drawing began. It could be noticed in the relief which spread amongst the townspeople when Bill Hutchinson drew the slip with the black dot. It could be seen in the faces of the Hutchinson children as they realized that they did not have the paper with the black dot. And it was confirmed in the fear and terror put forth by Tessie as the crowd descended upon her. The people that participated in the lottery had one purpose in mind--to survive.

A Sense of Finality Concluding Paragraph

This type of concluding paragraph is often used when the writer has organized the paper in an order of importance sequence. The final proof ends the paper and the writer indicates this by the choice of transition words.

> Finally, the worst mistake made by the man was his failure to take the old-timer's advice and not go alone on the Yukon trail. Obviously, since he journeyed alone, he had no one to help him when things became rough. The absence of a partner dominated over all his other mistakes. The young man's failure to use common sense caused his lonely, frozen death.

Quotation Concluding Paragraph

If you end your paper with a quotation concluding paragraph, make sure that the quote blends in with the paper's purpose. Too frequently writers tend to "tag" on a quote without explaining its significance. A quotation, used properly, capsulizes the thrust of the paper if it comes from a reliable source, especially if the quote reinforces your subject through the words of an "expert."

> The best example of hopeless monotony can be found at the very end of the book where Solzhenitsyn sums it up by saying,
>
> "There were three thousand six hundred and fifty-three days like this in his sentence, from reveille to lights out.
>
> "The extra ones were because of leap year . . ."

Here are two additional concluding paragraphs which end in a quotation. They both provide an emotional impact and capsulize the controlling idea for each composition.

Characterization of Julius Caesar

Shakespeare reveals the characterization of Julius Caesar in several ways. Caesar's impression of himself gives some ideas as to what his attitude would be like towards others. Since a character's deepest feelings are often revealed in his actions towards those close to him, Caesar's marriage to Calpurnia and relationship with his friends are brought into the picture. A character's true personality is often revealed in the way he treats those whom he has no special relationship with; therefore, Caesar's efficiency as a leader of the Roman people and their opinion of him is used to round out this characterization. An accurate statement of Caesar's ability as a leader as well as a character might be Mark Antony's final comment in Caesar's eulogy:

"Here was a Caesar! When comes such another?" III, 2, 246

The Theme of Loneliness from *Of Mice and Men*

In the novel *Of Mice and Men* Steinbeck showed the value of and the need for friendship. He also showed that man is not created for a lonely and isolated life, and no matter who he is, he needs others to be with. Crooks said it best: "A guy needs somebody--to be near him. Don't make no difference who the guy is, long's he's with you."

Evaluation Concluding Paragraph

This type of concluding paragraph ends with the writer supplying a personal comment and evaluation on the topic.

Human nature becomes frail in the face of difference or change. The new member becomes a "weak link" in the life chain. Through the expression of greed, guilt, and selfishness, the characters in *Flowers for Algernon* provide the ideal cameo of human nature, the fateful quality that cannot be escaped.

Here is another example of an evaluation concluding paragraph.

After the tragic death of his only child, Coyotito, Kino's whole world fell apart. Because of his greed and selfishness over the pearl, Kino had lost his son and had to start his whole life over again. The beautiful pearl with which he had hoped to buy happiness had now turned cold, grey, and ugly to him. With tears of sorrow in his eyes, Kino threw the pearl away.

WRITING AND LITERATURE

The five paragraph paper is the starting point for all major papers. The same principles that apply to the five paragraph paper apply to a paper of any length including a research project. First, think through your topic before "jotting down" ideas on your **Think Sheet**, establishing **short term goals** to accomplish.

Second, plan on the specific number of paragraphs you will write to support your controlling idea based on your short term goals. The number of paragraphs will vary depending on the scope of the assignment. At times you might expand or subtract ideas depending on your purpose. The main concern, however, is that you have thought through your subject and have planned on definite goals to be accomplished.

The *Of Mice and Men*, *Julius Caesar*, "The Most Dangerous Game," *Black Boy*, and *To Kill a Mockingbird* literature guides were prepared as complements to the **Stack the Deck** writing program. They take-up where the **Stack the Deck** organizational patterns end. The analytical, organizational, and writing skills learned are not only reinforced but enhanced by the added dimension of citation making.

You no longer will write from your own experience but examine a literary work to prove a thesis statement about one of its literary elements, such as a theme, tone, mood, characterization, symbolism, resulting in a marriage of the studies of writing and literature.

Besides offering another carefully sequenced "stacked deck" assignment for helping you improve your writing skills, another practical advantage is your gaining an understanding of literature by your writing about it.

INTRODUCTION--THEME

Basic to just about every story is an underlying idea from which an author can create characters, setting, and plot. This concept, theme, is so broad that often it can be stated in one abstract term. Thus we can say that the theme of Edgar Allan Poe's "Cask of Amontillado" is revenge, of John Steinbeck's *The Pearl* is greed, and of Jack London's "To Build a Fire" is the power of nature and the limitations of man.

Frequently you are able to detect the common theme of "Good wins over evil" in your viewing of television police stories. Despite the total differences of characters, settings, and plots involved in these shows, they all exhibit this common theme.

PREVIEWING EXERCISE

Read the following questions before you attempt to read John Steinbeck's *Of Mice and Men*. They will give specific details to look for and help you fill out the questions on **Citation Sheet** in your notebook.

1. Discuss the nature of themes as they apply to literature.
2. How are the themes of rootlessness and loneliness revealed in the book?
3. Identify other theme(s) in the novel even if they do not dominate.
4. What specific examples from the novel support your choice?
   To understand the theme of loneliness, you must understand how each character experienced loneliness.

   Use the following questions in analyzing each character.
5. What is the position (occupation) of each character? What does this reveal about this character?
6. What is the character's family background? What does this tell us about the character?
7. What sense of permanence does each character have?
8. What does this reveal about the character?
9. Who are the friends of each character? What does this reveal?
10. How does each person's physical appearance contribute to his/her loneliness?
11. How is each character viewed by the others in the novel? What does this reveal about the character? Does this contribute to the character's loneliness?
12. Which characters aren't **lonely**? Why?

CITATION (THINK) SHEET

Characters: As you are reading the novel, jot down ideas from your responses to questions 5 to 12 about each character's situation. Also, mark down the page numbers where you found your information. Your responses should be written on your own paper, not in the text.

1. George _____

2. Lennie _____

3. Candy _____

4. Crooks _____

5. Curley's wife _____

6. Curley _____

7. Slim _____

SUBJECT

In a multi-paragraph paper you will analyze the dominant theme of loneliness as it is reflected in the characters in John Steinbeck's *Of Mice and Men*. This may seem like a big task, but if you divide the paper into several (at least five) short term goals, it will not seem so difficult. You do this by deciding on several characters (at least three) and explain how they suffer from and express loneliness.

Your other two divisions will be an introductory paragraph and a concluding paragraph.

ALTERNATE TOPIC

Instead of analyzing the various characters and explaining how they epitomize the theme of loneliness, some of you might select the loneliest character in the novel. You must provide examples of why this character is the loneliest one in your analysis.

You would be writing an enumeration paper, that is, listing specific reasons to support your controlling idea. Your answers from the previewing exercise would be the content for the body of your composition.

Your controlling idea would have to state specifically whom you consider to be the loneliest character. Your ending might be a commentary, or you may even supply an appropriate quotation from the novel that captures the novel's theme.

Your teacher will decide which of these two assignments is appropriate for you.

ORGANIZATION

Since this is a multi-paragraph development, each developmental paragraph should discuss the loneliness of one of the characters. As in single paragraph development papers, each developmental paragraph must have its own controlling idea, method of organization, transition words for coherence, and ending. A full and complete explanation of each character's loneliness should be the heart of the paragraph.

By selecting three or four characters to write about, you will have solved the most difficult part of the assignment--deciding on the paper's content. Your specific answers to questions 5 through 12 from the previewing exercise and **Citation Sheet** should be the specific ideas to include in each paragraph. It is important, however, that you organize each developmental paragraph in some logical order. This organization will help you determine the transition words used to link your ideas.

By planning your paper in this fashion, you will be accomplishing short term goals. It is much easier doing it this way than in setting your sights on 500 or 1,000 word papers and having no specific direction.

Another major decision you must make is on how you are going to organize the sequence of your developmental paragraphs. One way would be to organize them in a degree of loneliness outline based on your interpretation of each character's loneliness. The choice is yours.

GLUING TOGETHER IDEAS

Each of your developmental paragraphs must be linked with the preceding paragraph. This can be accomplished by the repetition of the key word in your paper, in this case "loneliness," or by using some transition words that indicate a shift in supportive statements.

INTRODUCTORY and CONCLUDING PARAGRAPHS

You are expected to write an introductory paragraph and a concluding paragraph for this paper. Nothing has been mentioned about this until now because your emphasis should first be on the content of the paper. It is much easier to think about writing an introductory paragraph and a concluding paragraph once you have decided on the basic content and have had an opportunity to clarify your ideas.

Your introductory paragraph should try to accomplish the following:

1. Capture reader interest.
2. Introduce the subject.
3. Set the direction for your paper.

For this paper you have two types of introductory paragraphs to choose from: a quotation or a definition.

If you select a quotation introductory paragraph, pick out an appropriate quotation from the novel that captures the essence of what your paper is all about. However, be sure to relate the importance of the quotation and blend it in with the controlling idea of your introductory paragraph.

A definition introductory paragraph is also a good choice for this paper. First, you define the general term and then relate it to the specific subject of your paper. In this way you funnel down a general idea and clarify your subject to your reader.

Your concluding paragraph should end with a sense of finality, letting your reader know that you have written all there is to be written about your subject. Since your developmental paragraphs will be about the loneliness of several characters in the novel, you might end by summarizing and evaluating the main ideas discussed.

You may also conclude by leaving the most "severely tortured" person for last in a degree of loneliness organization. The appropriate glue or transition words would indicate that your paper is completed.

Refer to **Unit 18** for model introductory paragraphs and concluding paragraphs.

THINK SHEETS

Your **Citation Sheet** from the previewing exercise could serve as your **Think Sheet** for this paper. Make sure that you have completely exhausted your ideas. On a separate sheet of paper, reorganize your ideas for each character. The content will serve as the body of your composition.

Once you have organized the body of your composition, decide upon the appropriate introductory paragraph and concluding paragraph for your literary analysis.

INTRODUCTION-CHARACTERIZAQTION

William Shakespeare was not only a great playwright but also a master psychologist. He understood the workings of the human mind, even the dark recesses, and used this knowledge to create unforgettable characters. One way he was able to reveal the traits of characters was to show how two entirely different persons handled the same situation.

In William Shakespeare's *Julius Caesar*, Cassius and Brutus joined forces against Caesar because "he would be king," and together they promoted and executed the conspiracy against Caesar. Yet these two men were motivated by completely different psychological forces. Their common fear of Caesar thrust these entirely distinct personalities together. In normal circumstances they probably would never have been more than two Roman senators sharing the same title and nothing more.

PREVIEWING EXERCISE

In the discussion of such a complex play as *Julius Caesar*, you will go into many facets of the drama. However, keep these specific questions in mind. They will help you in gathering your material for a contrast paper dealing with the characters of Brutus and Cassius.

1. Why did Brutus and Cassius oppose Caesar?
2. What decisions were they required to make? How did they differ in arriving at the same decisions? Contrast the ease with which Cassius could make decisions with the difficulty Brutus experienced on these occasions:
   a. Caesar's assassination.
   b. Antony's speech at Caesar's funeral.
   c. Antony's death.
3. How did other characters in the play feel about them? Cite specific evidence from the dialogue.
4. Which of the two characters had more integrity? Why? What actions from the play support your position?
5. What character traits do each of them reveal in the dialogue and action? Cite specific textual quotes.
6. Which of the two is the more admirable character? Why?
7. Why did Cassius want Brutus in on the conspiracy? What does this reveal about both of them?

CITATION (THINK) SHEET

     Complete the **T-bar Citation Sheet** on a separate sheet of paper. When you jot down an idea for Brutus in response to the questions from the previewing exercise, jot down a corresponding idea for Cassius. Cite specific references from the play, whenever possible. Mark down the act, scene, and line. This will help you when you are working on the content for your paper.

BRUTUS	CASSIUS
1.	1.
2.	2.
3.	3.
4.	4.
5.	5.
6.	6.
7.	7.
8.	8.

SUBJECT

The subject of this paper is to analyze the differences between Brutus and Cassius, thus revealing what types of persons they were. Despite the fact that they joined together in the conspiracy, they differed in motivation, decision making ability, integrity, and worth or attractiveness as human beings. In your paper you should analyze the differences between Cassius and Brutus in at least three of these areas.

ORGANIZATION

As you answered the questions for the **Citation Sheet**, you became aware of many of these differences and jotted them down using a T-bar. Check your T-bar to see if it is sufficiently developed with specific citations from the play and to see if you can begin blocking off items into some common categories.

In organizing the body of your paper, you have two choices: the block method or flip-flop method. The following diagrams should prove helpful to you in organizing your paper:

	BLOCK		**FLIP-FLOP**
I	Introductory Paragraph	I	Introductory Paragraph
II	Block A Cassius	II	Topic A
III	Block B Cassius		Cassius
IV	Block C Cassius		Brutus
V	Block A Brutus	III	Topic B
VI	Block B Brutus		Cassius
VII	Block C Brutus		Brutus
VIII	Concluding Paragraph	IV	Topic C
			Cassius
			Brutus
		V	Concluding Paragraph

Each paragraph should contain a complete analysis of one of the major differences between Brutus and Cassius whether you use the block or flip-flop method of organization. Use quotations to support your ideas.

You must also plan an overall strategy for your paper. Which difference will you write about first? Will you organize in an order of importance sequence? Will you organize the ideas chronologically as they occurred in the play?

GLUING TOGETHER IDEAS

In writing a comparison/contrast paper, be aware of various methods of gluing together ideas. One method is by using transition words that show similarities or that point out differences.

Transition words for similarities: similarly, likewise, in the same manner, again, also, another, besides, furthermore, too.

Transition words for differences: although, as if, but, however, instead, on the other hand, yet, whereas.

Another way of gluing together ideas is to repeat similar sentence patterns or to repeat key phrases. This not only links ideas but also creates impact through the repetition of the key words.

Also, make sure that you link the developmental paragraphs. This can be accomplished by the repetition of a key idea.

INTRODUCTORY and CONCLUDING PARAGRAPHS

You may use a background information, quotation, or direct statement of fact introductory paragraph. If you use a direct statement of fact introductory paragraph, you can introduce your topics by pointing all the surface similarities between Brutus and Cassius and then bouncing off them to go into their differences as part of your controlling idea.

Your concluding paragraph may be a summarization of the body of your paper. Use a sense of finality concluding paragraph if you have organized your analysis in an order of importance sequence.

Refer to **Unit 18** for model introductory paragraphs and concluding paragraphs.

THINK SHEET

Your **Citation Sheet** from the previewing exercise should serve as **Think Sheet** for this paper. Once you decide upon the basic organization of your paper, reorganize your ideas based on whether you will be using the block organization, the flip-flop organization, or a combination of the two.

INTRODUCTION--FORESHADOWING

In a tale of action and suspense such as in "The Most Dangerous Game," Richard Connell, the author, in order to give his reader a feeling of belief in the story, plants hints along the way to help the reader guess what is to come, but more importantly, to believe events which otherwise might be unbelievable. This is especially true when the story is such a bizarre and unlikely one as is "The Most Dangerous Game." This planting of hints is technically called foreshadowing.

PREVIEWING QUESTIONS

Read the following questions which will help you understand the technique of foreshadowing and how Connell has applied it to "The Most Dangerous Game." Answering these questions will also aid you in completing the **Citation Sheet**.

1. What is the significance of the name of the island?
2. What hints do the following quotations give?
   a. "Sailors have a curious dread of the place."
   b. "This place has an evil name among seafaring men, sir."
   c. "An evil place can, so to speak, broadcast vibrations of evil."
3. What do you sense from Rainsford's and Whitney's discussing jaguar hunting?
4. What extremely unusual things on and around the island create a sense of mystery?
5. What does Rainsford see, hear, and discover that suggests the bizarre nature of the hunt?
6. What is revealed about Zaroff's feelings regarding hunting by the dinner table conversation?
7. What do you discover about Zaroff which might explain his extreme opinion about the hunt?
8. What does Zaroff's relationship with Ivan reveal about Zaroff?
9. What does Zaroff's telling about his hunting experience reveal about him?

CITATION (THINK) SHEET

Examples of foreshadowing from the setting   Details

1. _____

_____

2. _____

_____

3. _____

_____

Rainsford's discoveries   Their meaning (interpretation)

1. _____

_____

2. _____

_____

3. _____

_____

Zaroff's background and conversation   Their meaning (interpretation)

1. _____

_____

2. _____

_____

3. _____

SUBJECT

Richard Connell has created an unlikely, bizarre story in which a man becomes the ultimate game in the sport of hunting. In order to involve the reader in such a far-out situation, Connell spends a great deal of time in creating a sense of suspense and mystery in the first part of the story before he reveals the sinister plot of General Zaroff to use Rainsford as the prey in his next hunting expedition on Ship Trap Island.

Connell creates suspense and mystery by the description of Ship Trap Island and its surrounds, by the discoveries of Rainsford, and the revelation of Zaroff's background. He does this by giving us hints or clues which give the second part of the story believability. These hunts or clues are called foreshadowing.

Foreshadowing, then, is a literary technique by which the author gives the reader a suggestion of indication of an event before it actually takes place.

You will write a multi-paragraph paper in which you indicate how the clues listed in each of the section of your **Citation Sheet** create a sense of suspense and mystery and how these point to the fact that Rainsford will become the hunted and Zaroff the hunter.

ORGANIZATION

You may organize your developmental paragraphs chronologically as the story unfolds, or you many group your hints as they apply to Rainsford, Zaroff, and the setting (short term goals). You must fully explain the hints instead of merely listing them. Also make sure you show how these hints add to the story's believability, especially the final outcome. Do not retell the story--analyze.

Each of your main divisions could serve as a developmental paragraph. Make sure that each developmental paragraph is organized and includes necessary transitions.

GLUING TOGETHER IDEAS

Each of your developmental paragraphs must be linked with the preceding paragraph by using appropriate transition words or by repeating a key word or phrase that runs throughout the paper. These words might include *suspense*, *mystery*, *believability*, and *foreshadowing*.

INTRODUCTORY PARAGRAPH

You are expected to write an introductory and a concluding paragraph. Your introductory paragraph should accomplish the following:

1. Capture your reader's interest.
2. State the title and author of the story, properly punctuated.
3. Contain a controlling idea which indicates the direction of your paper.

This analysis would be an excellent one to begin with a quotation introductory paragraph or an incident introductory paragraph. Whichever type of introduction you select, it should capture the essence of your paper's subject and blend in with the controlling idea.

Other excellent choices include background information or a definition.

See **Unit 18** for models.

CONCLUDING PARAGRAPH

Your concluding paragraph should attempt to accomplish the following:
1. Leave the reader with an appreciation of Connell's use of foreshadowing.
2. Summarize the main idea.
3. Leave the reader with a sense of completion.

Since this analysis deals with Richard Connell's use of foreshadowing to add suspense and mystery to the story and to show how their use leads a careful reader to know ahead of time that Rainsford would be the hunted and Zaroff the hunter, your concluding paragraph may be an evaluation.

See **Unit 18** for different types of concluding paragraphs for literary analysis papers.

THINK SHEET

Your **Citation Sheet** from the previewing exercise serves as an excellent **Think Sheet** for this analysis. Make sure you have completely exhausted your ideas, supplying specific references from the story.

INTRODUCTION--BIOGRAPHY

In reading biography we learn many facts of a person's life. Among these are the influences in a person's surroundings which help form that person's character.

In Richard Wright's *Black Boy*, he reveals two dominating forces which were to leave a lasting effect on his person. These two forces were characterized by two segments of Southern society which victimized Richard during his formative years in the South and contributed to his eventual escape to the North, where he rebelled against both forms of oppression. These two segments were the dominating white and the consenting blacks. The dominating whites took every opportunity to put and keep Richard in his place, which was a role of subservience while the consenting blacks, motivated by fear, accepted and even defended this degrading condition.

PREVIEWING EXERCISE

Before reading Richard Wright's *Black Boy*, study the following questions so that you will be actively looking for material that will help you write a good paper. As you read the book, jot down items on your **Citation Sheet** and continue to do so as you discuss the book.

1. What was Richard's relationship with each of the following persons? What examples from their relationship can you cite to indicate their effect? What was the effect of each of these individuals on Richard?

a. Mother	e. Griggs	i. Pease and Reynolds
b. Aunt Addie	f. Father	j. Mr. Olin (Harrison)
c. Granny	g. Uncle Tom	k. Mr. Crane
d. Shorty	h. Uncle Haskins	

2. How did these events influence Richard?

a. The killing of Uncle Haskins	f. His speech as class
b. The hanging of Bob Greanley	valedictorian and his
c. Working for and white whites	encounter with the principal
d. Klu Klux Klan	g. Hanging the cat
e. His religious upbringing	

CITATION (THINK) SHEET

Directions: On a separate sheet of paper, complete the **Citation Sheet** as you are reading the book. Jot down ideas that support the basic theme of the book showing the indifference, cruelty, and subjugation Richard Wright experienced.

Character	Relationship	Example
1. Mother		
2. Aunt Addie		
3. Granny		
4. Shorty		
5. Griggs		
6. Father		
7. Uncle Tom		
8. Uncle Haskins		
9. Pease and Reynolds		
10. Mr. Olin (Harrison)		
11. Mr. Crane		

Event	Effect on Richard Wright
1. The killing of Uncle Haskins	
2. The hanging of Bob Greanley	
3. Working for and with whites	
4. KKK	
5. His religious upbringing	
6. His valedictory speech and encounter	
7. Hanging the cat	
8. Other	

SUBJECT

In a multi-paragraph paper you are to prove that the character of Richard Wright had been tremendously influenced by both dominating whites and consenting blacks in the South.

ORGANIZATION

You are to choose two or more specific examples of dominating whites and consenting blacks from your **Citation Sheet** to support your controlling idea. You have natural short term goals for organizing your analysis: dominating whites and consenting blacks.

You can deal with each of these using the block method, or you may write one paragraph on each of your items. If you choose the later, you might want to follow a flip-flop organization. Here is a model of each organizational design:

Introductory Paragraph	Introductory Paragraph
Block A	Flip A
Block B	Flop B
Concluding Paragraph	Flip A
	Flop B
	Concluding Paragraph

Each developmental paragraph should fully explore the character or event that helped form Richard Wright's character. Develop each paragraph sufficiently, citing facts, incidents, quotations for the book.

GLUING TOGETHER IDEAS

Each of your developmental paragraphs must be linked with the preceding one. This can be accomplished by using appropriate transition words that indicate a shift of ideas. You may also repeat a key word or phrase.

INTRODUCTORY PARAGRAPH

You introductory paragraph should accomplish the following:
1. Capture your reader's interest.
2. State the title and author of the book.
3. Contain the controlling idea, indicating your paper's direction.

A quotation or incident introductory paragraph must be an excellent choice for this assignment.

CONCLUDING PARAGRAPH

Since this analysis will deal with Richard Wright's condemnation of two segments of society, your concluding paragraph may be an evaluative comment of the society. You many choose to use a quotation which not only captures' the main thrust of your paper but also has a sense of finality.

Unit 18 contains examples of different types of introductory and concluding paragraphs.

THINK SHEET

Your **Citation Sheet** from the previewing exercise could serve as your **Think Sheet** for this analysis. Make sure you completely exhaust the ideas from the book.

INTRODUCTION--THEME

When was the last time you were really angry with someone? What did that person do or say that made you steaming mad? Parents are often prime targets for anger. Perhaps they wouldn't let you go to a party, allow you to do what everyone else was doing, or buy something you really wanted.

Now what do you suppose made your parents act that way? Were they simply being mean? Was there a reason or excuse for their behavior? Is it easier to understand a person when you try to understand things from his point of view?

On a larger scale, we sometimes fail to understand why another country or culture acts the way it does. How did the Iranians justify the taking of the American Embassy? Even though you may not have agreed with their actions, can you understand why they acted or felt the way they did?

Perhaps you can even think of a time when your actions or words were completely misunderstood by someone else. Maybe you even wanted to explain to that person why you did what you did so he could understand you better.

Along the same vein, the novel *To Kill a Mockingbird* deals repeatedly with being able to understand things from another person's point of view. "A thematic passage" is a statement or reflection about life or people in general. It is an idea with universal application, an idea that can be lifted from the novel and applied to the world outside the novel.

A major theme of *To Kill a Mockingbird* is that of compassion and understanding as illustrated by the thematic passage, "You never really understand a person until you consider things from his point of view . . . until you climb into his skin and walk around in it."

Discuss specific times when you were angry with someone. How did that other person feel? Try to "climb into that person's skin" and see his position.

PREVIEWING EXERCISE

The following questions should be considered as you read the novel. We will also discuss these in class. Thought given to these questions will help you in writing your assignment.

1. Why does the court appoint Atticus to defend Tom?
2. Which characters might be considered mockingbirds?
3. How much of Boo's strangeness is real? How much imagined?
4. How does Atticus try to change the children's attitudes?
5. How does Scout feel when she finally meets Boo and "stands in his shoes"?
6. Why was Tom convicted?
7. What trick does Atticus give Scout to help her understand people better?
8. Atticus says, "What Mr. Radley did might seem peculiar to us, but it did not seem peculiar to him." Explain how he can be justified in saying this and what he expects Scout to understand.
9. What do the children realize about Boo at the end of Chapter 8?
10. What did Jem understand about Mrs. DuBose as a result of his experience with her?
11. Why did Atticus unbutton his collar and loosen his vest during the closing arguments to the jury?
12. Atticus asks Jem to stand in Bob Ewell's shoes. What new insight does Jem gain by doing this?
13. What does the story of "The Gray Ghost" remind you of?
14. What did Scout realize when she stood on the Radley porch?
15. How do you feel about Mayella Ewell? Why does Scout call her the loneliest person in the world?
16. Why might the ladies of Maycomb Circle be considered hypocritical?

CITATION (THINK) SHEET

Directions: List examples of how each character had an opportunity to understand an incident from someone else's point of view. Because of your own unique insight, you may realize something which, at the time, the character did not fully grasp. You may quote what the character himself said, what was said to him, or what specific happenings occurred in the incident.

1. Jem_____

_____

_____

2. Scout_____

_____

_____

3. Dill_____

_____

_____

4. Miss Maudie_____

_____

_____

5. Atticus_____

_____

_____

SUBJECT

In a multi-paragraph paper you will analyze the theme of compassion and understanding. Many of the characters have several opportunities to understand things from another's point of view. You are to discuss at least three or more incidents that reflect this theme. In addition, you are to have an introduction and a conclusion.

ORGANIZATION

Each developmental paragraph should discuss an incident in which a character had an opportunity to be compassionate and understanding. Your **Citation Sheet** will serve as your guide in supporting your examples.

To explain your thoughts fully, each paragraph must have its own controlling idea, method of organization, glue words for coherence, and ending. The paragraph should be organized from general to specific: experiences with another character that are not too personal, to experiences to draw upon the experiences of several characters, or to use only one character's experience.

GLUING TOGETHER IDEAS

Each developmental paragraph must be linked with its preceding paragraph. Glue words will help to make your changes in ideas smooth. Here are some glue (transitional) words:

> also, another, as a result, at last, for example,
> for instance, furthermore, in addition, thus, too

You may also link your developmental paragraphs by repeating a key phrase or statement from the preceding paragraph.

INTRODUCTORY AND CONCLUDING PARAGRAPHS

Your introductory and concluding paragraphs are to be written after you complete your developmental paragraphs. Your introductory paragraph should be based on the quotation of the thematic passage. You must explain how the quotation serves as the controlling idea for your paper.

Your concluding paragraph should summarize the main points discussed.

Unit 18 includes model introductory and concluding paragraphs.

Punctuation Rules for Dialogue

1. Begin a new paragraph each time the speaker changes.

    "Hello," she said huskily.

    Only his brain answered, "Hi, Gorgeous."

    "Is anyone on the line?" she whispered.

    "I think so," he croaked.

2. Place quotation marks around the speaker's exact words. Quotation marks are not needed for indirect quotes--not the speaker's exact words.

    Direct quotation: "I will never speak to you again!" yelled Margie.

    Indirect quotation: Margie said that she would never speak to me again.

3. Begin a direct quote with a capital letter.

    "Jump in, Janice," commanded the dog's owner.

    The dog's owner commanded, "Jump in, Janice."

4. When the quotation is interrupted by a non-quoted expression such as "she replied," "he shouted," etc., the second part begins with a small letter.

    "Swinging from the bridge railing," he said, "is only asking for trouble."

    If the second part of a broken quotation is a new sentence, it should start with a capital letter.

    "The game has just started," Cassie explained. "You should be able to see most of it."

5. A direct quotation is set off from the rest of the sentence by commas.

    "Never, never ask me," Oscar exclaimed, "if you may borrow my mirror again. You've broken it." (Notice that no new quotation marks are needed when a new sentence is a part of the same quotation.)

6. Other marks of punctuation used with quotation marks are placed according to the following rules.

    A. Commas and periods are always placed inside the closing quotation marks.

       "The little gray cat," Mary Frances cried, "was my favorite kitty."

    B. Colons and semicolons are always placed outside the closing quotation marks.

       Mr. Fiske told us, "You have won the championship"; what he said after that I was too excited to hear.

       In the words of Mr. Fiske, the following students have "exceeded all our dreams": Jeni Finkbinder, Susan Lysander, Kenton MacCorum, and Dennis Townsend.

    C. Question marks and exclamation points are placed inside the closing quotation marks if the quotation is a question or an exclamation. Otherwise they are placed outside.

       "Are the contestants prepared?" asked the judge.

       "Yippee, ride 'em, cowboy!" hollered the eager fan.

    D. No more than one comma or one end mark is used at the end of a quotation.

       "Who," growled the captain, "said, 'Push the scurvy limey overboard'?"   (question mark only)

7. When a quoted passage consists of more than one paragraph, place quotation marks at the beginning of each paragraph and at the end of the entire passage, not at the end of each paragraph.

CORRECTION SYMBOLS
FOR REVISING AND PROOFREADING

abr..................................... abbreviation needed or abused

awk .... awkward sentence structure

beginning.......................... need a *catchy* opening

cap..................................... capitalization

combine .... **combine** sentences for variety

dm or **mm** .... dangling or misplaced modifier

ending............................... need a *pizzazz* ending; not *The End*

expand .... **expand** using journalistic questions

focus................................. no clear main idea

frag .... sentence fragment

gap .... a word is missing

^ .... insert a word

log .... not logical

org..................................... no organization; need a plan

.... new paragraph needed

punc .... punctuation

?... confusing

rearrange .... **rearrange** sentence parts

ref...................................... reference unclear

rep..................................... repetition; **subtract**

ro....................................... run-on sentence

seq .... ideas out of order; sequence properly

sp....................................... spelling

spec .... not specific enough; **expand**

subtract .... **subtract** the yuk

trans.................................. jumbled ideas; need a transition

var..................................... vary your sentences; **combine** and **rearrange**

vp .... verb power

vt .... verb tense inconsistency

wc...................................... word choice

yuk .... too wordy, subtract